wild tales from the police blotter

wild tales from the police blotter

C. J. Sullivan

THE LYONS PRESS
Guilford, Connecticut
AN IMPRINT OF THE GLOBE PEQUOT PRESS

The Lyons Press is an imprint of the Globe Pequot Press.

Text design by Claire Zoghb

Library of Congress Cataloging-in-Publication Data
is available on file.

ISBN 978-1-59921-134-3

Printed in the United States of America

10 9 8 7 6 5 4 3 2 1

dedication

To my daughters
Olivia and Luisa Sullivan:
you have made me a better
man for being in my life.
I love you.

Thank you to the
New York Post
for all of the fun and work we have had.

contents

introduction

AS A REPORTER FOR THE *New York Post*, and having worked in law enforcement in the courts of Brooklyn Supreme Court in New York City, the police blotter has long been my fascination, as it is for many other people. It's a barometer of human behavior, and often a yardstick of the strange and surreal.

If there's one thing I've learned from years as a beat writer and member of law enforcement, it's how easily people judge a cop on patrol. Until you've pulled over a car with tinted windows on a dark city street at 2:00 a.m. in the dead of winter, or seen the muzzle of a shotgun pointed at you, or been the first to arrive at a murder scene, you can't really know what you'd do, think, or feel in uniform. We've all heard the clichés, left and right: *Hey, officer, why you hassling me?* and *There's never a cop around when you need one.* But I for one appreciate that "thin blue line" between me and those people who would do me harm; more often than not, it's okay with me if that line's a little thicker than thin.

In this book I didn't want to deal with just the usual nitty-gritty badness cops come up against—although a lot of that made it into the book. What I also tried to do here was show the wild and wooly calls a cop gets on any given day—the stuff that makes the blotter get a little weird. Not just the robbery or car-accident calls, but the pet-tiger-gone-crazy call, or the millionaire-sports-hero-gone-crazy call.

Cops in this book face down aliens and crazed vigilantes. They deal with mobs out to avenge a friend's death and go after the wrong guy. They deal with hijackers and bootleggers and drug dealers and arms peddlers. They listen to the strangest stories that turn out to be true. They chase lights in the sky, not sure what the heck it is they are even chasing. They go up against alligators and bears and a whole slew of stupid criminals.

So crack open this book to any chapter, and sit back and enjoy a collection of tales that will make you laugh, make your hair curl, and probably make you look over your shoulder once or twice.

CHAPTER

1

gone missing

THE TRUE MYSTERY STORIES OF the police blotter are the reports of missing persons. In some of these incidents the person in question just doesn't want to be found. They skip town, blow the coop: A man or a woman fleeing an unhappy or abusive marriage. Debtors skipping out from under huge bills they can't find a way to pay. Teenagers looking for freedom. These stories can be met with cynicism; but there is no more heartbreaking police blotter story for a family, reporters, and cops than when a young child goes missing. It brings home every fear we have from the bogeyman stories of our childhood.

In January of 2007 one of the strangest stories on missing kids hit the police blotter. On Monday, January 8, a young, shy thirteen-year-old boy named William "Ben" Ownby stepped off a school bus in Beaufort, Missouri, a suburb of St. Louis. It was like he stepped off the end of the earth. He was gone, and the only break in the case was a white Nissan truck was seen speeding away from Ownby's last known location. This is one of those small details that sometimes break the biggest cases.

Ownby was a perfect victim for a child predator: small, quiet, and alone. But luckily for the child, on Friday, January 12, the white Nissan led the police and FBI to Kirkwood, Missouri—about an hour outside of St. Louis. At an apartment complex, Michael Devlin, forty-one, was arrested while taking out the garbage. FBI agent Ronald Covington entered the house and found two boys, one of them Ben Ownby. The child looked at the agent and asked, "Are you going to take me home?"

Covington said he would, and then he turned to the fifteen-year-old boy with Ownby and asked him who he was. The teenager said he was named Shawn Hornbeck. Hornbeck had been missing for more than four years.

"Oh, my God! That's my son!" Craig Akers told reporters when he saw his missing stepson. Shawn had longer and darker hair, was much taller, and had a pierced lip when he was found.

Hornbeck was eleven when he went missing in October of 2002. His parents had quit their jobs and depleted all their savings searching for the child, including setting up a Web site to aid the search. His photo was everywhere, with the legend that he was missing. His parents never lost hope, even though the FBI had told them that Shawn Hornbeck was likely dead. The FBI surmised that Hornbeck had been out riding his bike in Richwoods, another St. Louis suburb, on that fateful day in 2002 and likely had been hit by a car and the driver had disposed of his body in a ditch on the side of the road.

However, Hornbeck had been in plain sight for more than four years, and no one had reported it. Devlin, described by newspapers as a three-hundred-pound pizza parlor manager, had been rooming with Hornbeck, and no one thought it odd; some neighbors assumed he was Hornbeck's father, just another single dad raising a teenage son. Mike Prosperi, Devlin's boss and the owner of Imo's Pizza, claimed that Devlin had worked for him for fifteen years and was a great employee with no hint of any scandal in his life. Others agreed. Neighbors described him as a regular guy, and his landlord said he was one of his best tenants—he was quiet and paid his rent on time.

But Mike Devlin was also a busy man. Along with bizarre Web postings on sites visited by teenagers, he worked days flinging pizza pies and then pulled a night shift at a Kirkwood funeral home answering the phones. He had no police record—other than traffic violations—and the pizza shop he managed was near the Kirkwood police station. Devlin knew many of the local cops and buddied up with a few as he served them at the pizza parlor.

Neighbors at Devlin's Kirkwood apartment saw Shawn Hornbeck coming and going as he pleased. He was a skateboarder, and was alone most times. One neighbor saw Hornbeck bring a girl home, and others claimed that he drove Devlin's Nissan by himself. He was not enrolled in any school and he spent most of his time in the apartment playing video games—again, alone.

When the media started to wonder whether Hornbeck just didn't want to be found, his parents defended their child by saying that Devlin would have killed Hornbeck and the rest of his family if he talked. Others brought up the 2003 Salt Lake City, Utah, kidnapping of Elizabeth Smart, who lived nine months with her abductor and passed up many chances to escape. The Stockholm Syndrome—in which the abductee overly identifies with his or her keepers in order to survive—was invoked in Hornbeck's defense.

"You have to wonder why Shawn Hornbeck didn't try to escape after it seems he had great freedom for a very long time. There were few signs of trauma in this case," said Janon Fisher, a reporter who covered the Devlin-Hornbeck case for the *New York Post*. "But Devlin is a mystery. It doesn't appear that he did this for sex. In most child abduction cases where strangers are involved the motivation is sexual assault, molestation, or murder. None of that seems to have happened. So is Devlin a lonely bachelor who just wanted company? Was he a man-child with arrested development looking to pal around with teenage boys? Only Devlin knows the reason and hopefully it will all come out in court."

Michael Devlin is believed to have kidnapped boys before. He is currently being investigated for the abduction of Arlin Henderson, eleven, of Moscow Mills, Missouri, also a suburb of St. Louis, in July of 1991. No one ever saw Henderson again. Cops looking at this sixteen-year-old case were amazed at the similarities between it and the Devlin-Hornbeck case.

"If you were to take a photo of Arlin Henderson and place it next to Shawn Hornbeck's picture, there is a striking resemblance," Lieutenant Rick Harrell, of the Lincoln County Sheriff's Office, said to reporters.

Some of the most disturbing details about this case are the experiences of Shawn Hornbeck during his days of captivity. Ten months after he went missing, Hornbeck reported—alone—to a cop that his bike had been stolen. But he gave his name as Shawn Devlin. He didn't say anything about being the victim of a kidnapping.

The investigation also discovered that Hornbeck actually dated a freshman girl in the fall of 2006. She attended the Visitation Academy. He and the girl dated for months and were allowed complete freedom to come and go without Devlin being anywhere near them. One December, Hornbeck took the girl to a high-school dance at the St. Louis Priory School, where girls from Visitation went for a mixer.

When reports came out that Shawn was abducted, the girl was actually razzed about it at her school. The *New York Post* reported one of her classmates saying, "I know it's getting hard for her because everyone is giving her a hard time. They're saying, 'Oh, you must have known he was missing or had been abducted.' But, honestly, she had no idea."

As the story built momentum in the early months of 2007, reports surfaced stating that Hornbeck's biological father, Walter Hornbeck, was a convicted sex offender who did three years in a Missouri prison on drug and sodomy charges in 1994. The father had little contact with his son during this time and none after he got out of prison in 1997. He died of a heart attack in 2000. That might not mean a thing. But it leaves a person to wonder how having a deviant and criminal father might play into the mindset of an abducted teen.

When a *Post* reporter nabbed a jailhouse interview with Devlin on January 21, 2007, Devlin discussed his lack of interest in sex and said all he enjoyed in life was playing poker and video games. He complained that his longtime friends had all gotten married and he had few people to hang out with.

But at least he felt some shame for his crime. "I don't know how I'm going to explain myself to my parents," he said to the reporter. "It's much easier talking to a stranger about these things than your parents."

He wouldn't talk about the case but said, "I'm guess I was relatively happy. . . . I feel nothing. I hide my emotions from other people. I hide the way I feel. . . . I guess you could say I was lonely."

Devlin may have been lonely, but he wasn't alone. On January 24, 2007, KMOV, a local St. Louis TV station, released details from a report of an unnamed law enforcement source that Shawn Hornbeck helped Michael Devlin abduct Ben Ownby. The report stated that Hornbeck jumped out of Devlin's Nissan, grabbed Ownby, and forced him into the truck where Devlin held a gun to the younger boy and duct-taped him.

Franklin County Sheriff Gary Toelke would not deny or confirm these statements to the *St. Louis Dispatch* but did say, "This information doesn't need to be released right now. It's based on speculation. It's only harmful to the boys and their families."

A month later a source close to the investigation leaked to a local TV station that Shawn Hornbeck helped Devlin hide Ben Ownby when they first kidnapped the younger boy. The source said that it had to do with how Devlin snatched Hornbeck—hinting that he might have had yet another older boy in his lair when he grabbed Hornbeck in 2002.

KVTI-TV of St. Louis released photos of Hornbeck wearing a red bandanna over his face and pointing an automatic pistol at the camera. Psychologist and criminal profiler Lawrence Martin thought that the photo of Hornbeck with a gun was a turn-on for Devlin. Clearly, the kidnapping did something to Hornbeck's young mind that turned him into a performer and participant, roles that he might have hated but felt forced to take on.

Devlin's arrest has given other parents of missing children some kind of hope—however slim. As of the publishing of this book, Michael Devlin is in custody with $1 million bail on felony kidnapping charges, and the two boys are adjusting to their return to the relative freedom of American youth.

•••

This story was unusual not just because two boys were found together after abductions four years apart, but also because it ended with the victims alive. Many missing persons stories end badly, and hopes are dashed. Or, even worse, a case gets old, turns cold, and is never solved, and the parents never find out what happened to their children.

May 25, 1979 was a day that changed America when a missing persons story came off the New York City police blotter and then went national. This was before the days of missing child photos on milk cartoons. This disappearance played a large role in creating the missing child network that now operates coast to coast.

This missing person story began on a spring morning when a precocious six-year-old boy named Etan Patz woke up in his Prince Street apartment in the Soho district of Manhattan. After he dressed for school—he attended first grade—he finally convinced his mother, Julie, to let him walk the two blocks to the school bus by himself. Julie Patz had never before let Etan walk to school alone. She figured it was the end of the school year and he could handle it. The little boy said goodbye to his mother and walked out of the apartment with a blue school bag on his shoulder. He wore his beloved blue captain's cap and had one dollar in his pocket. It was the last time Julie Patz would ever see her son.

Somewhere on that two-block walk to West Broadway the streets swallowed Etan Patz whole. He was never heard from again. At this late date, Etan Patz would be thirty-three years old. The police have assumed he is dead.

In New York—and most of America—in 1979 it was not unusual to see six-year-olds walking to school by themselves. After the Patz case, it became a rare event. Concerned parents made sure that an adult dropped off and picked up their children from school directly.

The newspapers jumped all over the Patz case and turned it into a national sensation. Etan Patz became one of America's most visible missing kids. His picture and story ran daily in the tabloids. Five hundred cops worked on a task force to find the boy. More than 30,000 posters were handed out and posted in the city. Stan Patz, Etan's father, was a professional photographer and had numerous high-quality shots of his son. The picture that was used the most depicted a button-cute towheaded little white boy.

In the wake of Etan's disappearance, milk cartons became ad hoc wanted posters for lost kids. In 1983 President Ronald Reagan declared May 25 to be Missing Children Day, and on that night people throughout the country were encouraged to leave their porch lights on to show the vanished children the way home. Before 1979 there was no national data bank to document the 2,000 kids who go missing every year in America. Now there is one, and all this is because Etan Patz walked down a Soho street and was never seen again.

In 1982 the NYPD picked up a man named Jose Ramos near Jerome Avenue in the Bronx. Ramos was arrested for trying to lure young boys into an abandoned storage tunnel in which he was living deep in the woods of Van Cortlandt Park. The police tried to nail the Patz case on him but were unsuccessful. A cop working the case said that Ramos was an ugly, hunchbacked man who had a soft voice when speaking to kids. Ramos was freed on bail and fled New York. He bought himself an old school bus and used it to lure kids in for rides. He traveled the country and may have been responsible for quite a few molestation cases. But Ramos was smart and kept moving around.

Finally, in 1990 Ramos was arrested in Pennsylvania for molesting children. He received a twenty-year sentence. A jailhouse snitch once testified that Ramos told him, "Etan is dead. There is no body and there never will be a body."

In jail, Ramos reportedly once admitted that he had been friends with Etan's babysitter and took Etan to his apartment on May 25, 1979 but let him go unharmed. He later recanted that story, and since then has been in a Dallas, Pennsylvania, jail saying not much of anything. Especially not about Etan Patz.

Cops who could not go on the record for this book agreed that Ramos most likely had a hand in Patz's disappearance. Etan's dad, Stan Patz, also thinks Ramos killed his son. Twice a year—on Etan's birthday, October 9, and on May 25—Stan Patz sends Ramos a letter to his jail cell. He encloses a photo of Etan, and he always writes to Ramos, "What have you done to my little boy?"

A police officer in Pennsylvania, requesting anonymity, said, "I think Stan Patz should stop doing that. It is a futile gesture. It keeps Etan alive for that freak Ramos. He can sit in his jail cell and relive what he did to that kid like 1979 was yesterday. Child molesters frequently have these fantasies. As a father I would want revenge, but I wouldn't want Ramos looking at pictures of my son. He will not crack. Ramos is sixty and still won't talk. A photo won't make him start. It gives him his jollies when he gets that photo twice a year."

In 2001 Etan Patz was declared legally dead, and the Patz family won a summary judgment against Jose Ramos for a wrongful death lawsuit in civil court. Ramos came up for parole in 2004 and was denied his freedom. His next parole date was in 2007, with the same result. Julie and Stan Patz were there to make sure Ramos stayed in jail. Ramos might never again breathe air as a free man.

The body of Etan Patz has never been found.

•••

On August 12, 1985, on Briggs Avenue in the Bronx another child went missing. Yet no one worried about what happened up in the Bronx on that hot and cruel summer night. The story about this missing child never made it into the papers or TV news. No one cared except one good cop.

Equilla Hodrick, a pretty eight-year-old black girl, sat with her mother, Terona, on their apartment building steps that night. Terona was eight months pregnant and stoop-sitting with her daughter was about all she could manage. A few friends of Terona's stopped by to talk. When she turned to look back at her daughter, she saw Equilla running down Briggs Avenue and then making a left onto 194th Street.

"That was the last time I saw my baby," Terona Hodrick said. She still sighs when she speaks of her missing daughter. "I couldn't run after her because I was pregnant but I figured that she was just going down the block and would be back. My niece saw her later at a game room down the block but when it got later in the night I felt something was wrong and I called the police."

The cop who took the call was Detective Frankie McDonald, a seasoned eighteen-year veteran. Years later he talked about the case like it happened last week: "It was heart wrenching. The mother was a genuine victim and this was a legitimate missing child case. Many times in those cases another family member was involved. Not in this one."

The case has stayed with McDonald even though he is now retired from the NYPD. He moved on to the private sector to make more money and is now the head of security at Pace University. McDonald is a big, warm man with a cool head. In his twenty years as a cop he was shot at three times and never once fired his weapon back. "I was just lucky," is all he'll say about the shootings.

Terona Hodrick thought highly of Frankie McDonald's police work. "My family and I loved him. I named my son after him. He did everything he could," she said.

The 911 call reporting Equilla Hodrick's disappearance didn't cause much of a stir among residents of the Bronx. The NYPD, however, formed a massive search for the little girl.

"Our bloodhounds picked up Equilla's scent and they led us down to Webster Avenue by the tracks of the Metro-North line," McDonald said. "We had heard from the neighborhood people that a lot of homeless were camped out down there so we went to do a search."

There he ran into the Metro-North's railroad bureaucracy. It took McDonald hours to get through to Metro-North to get permission to search the tracks. The railroad didn't want to stop the trains because of the inconvenience to their commuters. McDonald let them know that the neighborhood might not like the fact that a train schedule came before a little girl's life.

"We never did get them to stop the trains. They only slowed them down. We looked for quite awhile but found nothing."

When McDonald got back to the 52nd Precinct, the search had become a news story. Only it wasn't over Equilla Hodrick's disappearance, but how some cop had slowed down the trains. A reporter from Channel 2 stuck a mike in McDonald's face and demanded to know who had made the decision to slow down the trains.

McDonald looked at the female reporter and said, "Nobody made that decision. We made the decision to search for a missing child. What is your story? That an eight-year-old girl is missing? Or that a few assholes from Westchester and Connecticut came home to a cold dinner?"

Years later, McDonald said, "The media gave this case no play. It only got press when we slowed down the trains. Very different from Etan Patz."

McDonald spent his last two years as a cop on the Hodrick case. He chased every lead, and nothing ever came of it. When he put in his papers to retire, he visited Terona Hodrick and told her he was turning in his badge. She sighed and said, "Well, that's the end of it."

"She was right. After I left there wasn't much more to be done," McDonald said. "Although every effort was made by the police department to find her daughter. Everything that could have been done was done. We tried. We really tried."

In agreement with McDonald, Terona Hodrick said, "The police searched every apartment building around here from Valentine Ave. to Webster. They really looked for Equilla and for that I am grateful."

As of 2007 the Equilla Hodrick case is still active. Terona Hodrick got a call from a newly formed cold case squad in the missing persons unit in 2001, but that came to nothing. She still has hope.

"I still pray that she will come home. I know in my heart that she is alive because I can feel her. You know how it is with a mother and her child. You can feel them. She's out there. I know she's not underground. Not my baby," Terona Hodrick said. If she's right, Equilla would turn thirty this year.

"I hate to upset the mother but I don't think [Equilla] is alive," Frankie McDonald said. "Equilla was very savvy for an eight-year-old. She knew her phone number. She was school smart and street smart. She would have reached out for the mother. She wasn't a troubled child and had a good relationship with her mother. If she could have called she would have."

Terona Hodrick refuses to believe that. She now lives on 101st Street and Columbus Avenue in Manhattan but always keeps her phone number listed.

"I had to get away from the Bronx. All those bad memories. I wound up here. Whenever I move I keep my name in the book. I have to so I can be reached. Someday I am going to hear from Equilla."

•••

After the Patz case America woke up to the need for tracking missing people—adults as well as children—and since 1979 missing people have become quite common. The FBI reports that it investigated more than 47,842 missing persons in 2006. In 30,622 of those cases, people have been missing for more than a year. And 17,500 of these cases were people who were considered at great risk.

In addition, the National Crime Information Center (NCIC) has more than 6,000 unclaimed bodies waiting to be identified. Given that in 2006 the FBI had 30,626 employees—fewer than the NYPD—and is investigating more than 12,000 fugitives along with all those missing persons, getting to the bottom of these cases can be tough.

The FBI numbers are just the tip of a very big iceberg. The state of California alone reports more than 25,000 active missing person cases and more than 2,100 unidentified bodies in its database.

"With a missing person, time is so important," an NYPD veteran said. "In a lot of these cases someone just wants to be missing, and with the kids it usually is an estranged parent who grabs the kid to get back at the other parent. But when it is an out and out mystery it is a tough thing to solve. A lot of these cases we get are just bullshit—some guy ducking under the radar to avoid paying alimony or child support—but the real ones will break your heart."

This officer, who requested anonymity, told a classic missing person story: A twenty-one-year-old Texas woman was having trouble with her grades in college. She wanted to drop out of school and go to work, but her parents objected. They wanted her to stay in school. Over the Christmas break she pleaded with them to let her leave school, but they would not bend. She went back to campus, packed a bag, and disappeared.

As the years went by, the parents became convinced that their child was dead. In ten years they hadn't heard a word from her. No clue of her whereabouts ever surfaced. But she was not dead; she had moved to Kentucky and started working at a Sam's Club. She worked under her own name and Social Security number but did not take out any credit cards, and her roommates held the lease for their apartment and paid for the utilities.

The cop said this woman was only discovered when she applied for a Kentucky driver's license. The motor vehicle hit alerted the Texas authorities, and the family went to Kentucky to reunite with their now thirty-one-year-old child. The daughter and parents marveled over how they had all aged in the intervening decade.

"Most of these cases don't have such a neat and happy ending," the cop said.

•••

Investigator Ken Richards, who runs a missing persons Web site, says, "In my own research I learned that there is no greater asset in the search for missing persons than the consistent distribution of information through every available means."

One way to get the information out is via the Internet. The Web site for the National Center for Missing Adults lists 1,394 people on its database. The first name on the list is Leigh Abel, seventy-eight, who went missing in 2001 in Orange City, Florida. Old Leigh was out fishing for sea bass at New Smyra Beach near his house. He packed up his gear, got into his truck, and was never seen again. A few days later his truck was found a mile from the beach, but there was no sign of Leigh Abel. The site posts a composite picture of an unidentified young man who may know what became of him. The last entry on the site is Jeff Zoltawaski, who was twenty-three in 1993 when he went missing while hiking in his hometown of Wallua, Hawaii.

Paging through these cases online brings you to one troubling mystery after another. An entire police force or federal agency could be tied up for years trying to clear them.

The San Francisco Police Department has a busy missing persons squad. One case that continues to baffle those officers dates from 2003. In a photo, Ann-Marie Lawrence, twenty-nine, appears to be a happy and smiling bleached blonde. She went missing on November 22, 2003. A friend dropped Lawrence off on the 2400 block of Fulton Street. But she never went into her apartment. Instead she ran across the street into Golden Gate Park, and that was the last that was ever seen of her. She has family in southern California, but no one has ever heard from her. I called Inspector Gordon and she had no information on the Lawrence case. Without trying to cast aspersions on the cops, that is what happens to most missing persons' files: they sit in a closet, dust settles, and they're forgotten by the next generation of police.

Another American city that has a missing persons problem is Houston, Texas, which has more than 7,000 open cases. Sergeant Stuart Harris heads that city's missing persons squad and bemoans the fact that he has only nine investigators for this caseload. Harris admits that many of the cases are runaways and child custody cases—but not all. He told TV station KHOU, "Missing persons tend to rank down on the bottom of the priority list, unfortunately."

•••

Missing persons are a worldwide problem. They are called "mispers" in the United Kingdom.

On the cool early spring afternoon of March 26, 1993, Annie McCarrick, twenty-six and a Long Island native who had been living in Ireland for three months, left her Sandymount, Dublin, apartment to pick up her paycheck at Café Java and then went shopping for groceries.

When she got back to her flat, she put away her groceries and set about washing her lingerie in the sink. She called a friend to see if she wanted to go listen to some music at Johnny Fox's Pub in Enniskerry. The friend declined the offer, and a few hours later McCarrick walked out her front door alone and was never seen again.

To the Irish police, Annie McCarrick had merely "gone missing" and would turn up again. They told her worried parents that maybe Annie just went for a wander, and when she was done with it she'd come back home. She never did.

Her frantic parents pushed the issue for years. The longer it went on, the more they came to believe their daughter had become the victim of a crime and she would never be heard from again because she was dead and buried in some Irish bog, and not much was being done about it.

The U.S. Embassy got involved, and when five other young women in the same Dublin-Wicklow-Kildare area "went missing" after McCarrick, the Garda (the Irish police) realized they might have had a serial killer on their hands. Frighteningly, women have frequently "gone missing" in Ireland for the last twenty years, and not all of them have stayed in the foggy land of the unknown. Wooded areas, bogs, garbage dumps, and peat holes have coughed up the bodies of a few murdered women, and no one knows if any of them are connected.

John McCarrick, Annie's father, was willing to talk about his daughter, who's been missing for more than fourteen years. He wanted her story told, and he longed to find out what happened to his beloved daughter.

"During Annie's sophomore year at Skidmore College she took a student trip to Ireland and fell in love with the country," he said. "She went in 1987 to live in Ireland because she felt like there were less bad influences there. She got her degree at St. Patrick's."

In 1990 Annie went back to New York to get her master's degree in English at Stonybrook. But by January of 1993 she moved back to Ireland. She found a nice apartment right near the water, her father said. She was working in a place called Café Java baking pies. "She loved to cook."

"The last time I talked to Annie was on March 21, 1993. She was in good spirits," her father said. "On the twenty-sixth I found out she had picked up her pay at Café Java and delivered some pies for them. I think after that she did some shopping. Later on she supposedly got on a bus to Enniskerry to go to a bar called Johnny Fox's Pub. I guess she wanted to go there because they play traditional Irish music.

"We found out she was missing by a call from one of her friends. They were going to have dinner with her the next night and knew something was up when she hadn't returned home. Right away I thought something was wrong. My wife was on a plane to Ireland the next day. I followed her two days later. By Tuesday I was in Ireland looking for Annie. My wife had been planning on visiting her in early April and there was an itinerary and theater tickets lying around the apartment. She had my wife's visit all planned out. Annie had everything to live for. I knew she didn't just go missing."

The McCarricks encountered a less-than-stellar police response.

"The first Irish cop we talked to took notes on his hands," McCarrick says. "It took us two weeks to get any real police action. We made up posters and plastered the route from Sandymount through the Wicklow Mountains. You ever see the road from the Wicklow Mountains to Dublin? It's deserted, dark, and lonely. If she went to that pub and hitchhiked back . . ."

The Wicklow Mountains are about twenty miles southwest of Dublin. It's a wild and rough land, and parts of it are impenetrable. The ground is covered by gorse and heather, and the mountains are a series of hills and peaks. The wooded glens are very secluded.

The McCarricks got U.S. Ambassador Jean Kennedy Smith to nudge the Garda to take the case seriously. The missing woman's father and mother also hired an Irish private detective. But no one found a clue. The McCarricks posted a $125,000 reward for information that would help solve Annie's case. "All we got out of that were a bunch of loonies calling," John McCarrick said. "Not one serious call."

Since Annie McCarrick went missing, five other women have disappeared from the same area of Dublin. In 1998 Garda Commissioner Pat Byrne told the *Irish Times* that the police were addressing the possibility that one person might have killed Annie and others. It took a lot to get the Irish cops to admit that a serial killer might be at work in a country that likes to boast to tourists that they have one of the lowest crime rates in the western world. Commissioner Byrne said the police were assuming that all six women were dead, and that they were victims of either murder or manslaughter.

"We have no bodies, which means that we have no crime scene and that in itself is a tremendous disadvantage," Byrne said at the time. "We want to find out if they were enticed or if they were forced from where they were last seen. It is unclear whether they were killed by one person or more."

Asked if he suspected the existence of a serial killer, Byrne said, "It is an aspect that is being considered. We have to find out whether two or three of these murders are related."

According to her father, when Annie went out that last day, she was wearing an antique Rolex watch and carrying her credit cards and wallet. None of those items has ever surfaced. All of her bankbooks, her passport, and her personal possessions were still in her apartment. Clearly, she was not fleeing the country or taking a sudden flight to New York. Her departure was not planned. Maybe she was simply the victim of an accident, or amnesia?

In 1995 when the Garda first started to look into Dublin's rash of missing and murdered women, it found that one man had relationships with two women who had been murdered in the early 1990s in Dublin. Until that time no cross-referencing of the murders or disappearances of women had been done. The man was arrested and admitted to killing both women by strangulation. They were cold-blooded killings. He received a ten-year sentence for manslaughter.

But in no way could this one killer have been responsible for all the missing women of Ireland. The following is a roll call of some of

"Pat the Ripper's" possible victims. As of 2007 none of these crimes have been solved.

The first may have been Phyllis Murphy, twenty-eight, who on a cold December evening in 1979 was last seen walking on a road near Roseberry. A few weeks later her body was found in the Wicklow Gap, strangled to death.

On April 3, 1988 the decomposed body of Antoinette Smith was found buried in a bog at Glendoo. Smith was last seen in July of 1987 leaving a David Bowie concert at Slane Castle in Dublin. She was raped and strangled.

Deirdre Mulcahy, nineteen, was found raped and strangled outside of Cork. This is the one murder that took place far from the others. A man was brought in for the crime, but he was later cleared of all charges. Mulcahy's death remains a mystery.

On December 23, 1991 Patricia Doherty disappeared after doing some Christmas shopping. Her body was found in Kilakee in a collapsed peat bank in July of 1992. This was about two miles from where Antoinette Smith was buried.

Annie McCarrick disappeared in March of 1993.

On July 23, 1993 Eva Brennan, forty, from South Dublin, left her parents' flat to return to her home. She was never heard from and is believed to be dead.

On December 16, 1993 Marie Kilmartin, thirty-six, from Portlaoise, went missing. Six months later her body was found in a bog with a concrete slab placed on her chest to hold her down.

On November 9, 1995 Jo-Jo Dullard was last seen at a telephone kiosk in Callen at about 11:30 p.m. It's believed she tried to hitch a ride home to her town of Moone. Her body probably lies somewhere in the mountains along the road where she was last seen.

Fiona Pender, twenty-five years old and seven months pregnant, went missing outside her Tullamore, County Offaly, home in August of 1996. No body was ever found.

Ciara Breen, eighteen, from Dundalk, was last seen in the town on February 12, 1997. She took no possessions with her as she left her home on Bachelor's Walk. She never returned.

Fiona Sinnott, nineteen and from Lady's Island, Wexford, left a local pub on February 8, 1998 and was never heard from again.

The last girl to go missing, on July 28 of 1998, was Deirdre Jacob, eighteen, last seen near the same spot from which Phyllis Murphy had been snatched from nineteen years earlier. Some veteran Garda recalled the earlier murder and thought the similarity was eerie. Jacob's body has not been found.

In 2004 Gerry O'Carroll, a highly decorated Irish detective, spoke on the cases of the missing Irish woman. "The facts speak for themselves. For decades we have had virtually no missing women, now we have up to ten in a relatively small area around the east coast with various common threads. I believe these women were victims of one or two serial killers working together."

And that is where it ends for now. Since 2000 six other women have gone missing from the area where Annie McCarrick disappeared, but as no bodies have been found, the cases sit in file drawers, getting colder and colder.

CHAPTER 2

serial killers

EVER SINCE AN FBI AGENT named Robert Ressler coined the term "serial killer," stories of such murderers have been something of an obsession for many Americans. From movies like *Se7en* and *Silence of the Lambs* to TV shows like *Criminal Minds*, America seems curiously fascinated by serial killers.

While police blotters across the country and through the years have lit up with serial killer cases, there are some in particular that scare the hell out of the citizens of the city where the murders take place. Panic hits the street when these stories break, and while it is more likely that a person would be killed in a car accident than by a serial killer, these tales of murder and mayhem pierce deep into the psyche—as if our worst nightmares have come to haunt our waking hours.

The following serial killers that littered the police blotter were able to get into different people's heads in various cities and terrify the people who lived there. The stories became bigger than crime itself. For example, in 2006 four prostitutes were killed in Atlantic City, New Jersey, and the bodies were all laid together in a drainage ditch right outside the gambling mecca of the East Coast. That four women could be murdered so callously and then dumped together in a ditch without one eyewitness sent a shiver down the spines of the denizens of that oceanside city.

Then there was the horrific case of Jeffrey Dahmer, who killed seventeen men in and around the Milwaukee area, and after killing his victims he would sometimes dine on their remains. When that story hit the police blotter, the people of Milwaukee were horrified. After he was tried and convicted, Dahmer's house was leveled to the ground by bulldozers, as if Milwaukee was exorcizing itself of the stench of Dahmer's life.

The demonically named killer Son of Sam put New York City in a mode of high-alert fear in 1977. Son of Sam may have been copying an earlier killer in San Francisco named the Zodiac Killer. Zodiac was never caught, and he taunted the City by the Bay for years with his weird letters to newspapers. His writing alone kept people in fear for their lives. Son of Sam used the same trick of writing to newspapers to get publicity. The San Francisco Zodiac had another copycat killer who plied his trade in New York in 1990, and he turned the city on its head with worrying about who would be next.

Coral Watts terrorized Ann Arbor, Michigan, in the late 1970s and then took his killing trade to Texas when he felt like the cops were closing in. The coeds of Ann Arbor and the women in Texas lived in fear of being his next victim.

Strangely, Ann Arbor, Michigan, seems to attract serial killers. Seven years before Coral Watts, another man, John Collins, killed six young female college students, and he, too, caused terrible fear in the town of Ann Arbor and surrounding communities. Ironically Collins was at his worst in 1967—the Summer of Love—when most collegians were talking about peace and love and Collins was singing a song of murder.

All wrong.

These serial killers also have luck in common. Some were never caught—by pure dumb luck—and the others were caught only through hard work by police and some lucky breaks that the cops caught along the way.

•••

On November 20, 2006 four women were found dead in a drainage ditch right outside the border of Atlantic City, New Jersey. Now, Atlantic City—like its gambling sister city, Las Vegas—does not want the press that a multiple murder brings. The police blotter was full of speculation about a serial killer prowling the dark edges of a town that kept gambling, drug dens, and prostitution in business.

This was an odd case for the police. Links and coincidences leapt out at detectives, and some cops said—off the record—that it was like they were being taunted. It was almost as if the killer was daring them to catch him. All four women were blonde. They all had their shoes and socks or stockings removed. All of their heads were pointed east in the direction of the casinos on the boardwalk of Atlantic City. They all were placed facedown in a few inches of water—possibly to wash away any DNA evidence—in a drainage ditch behind a seedy strip of fifteen-dollar-a-night motels on Route 322 in Egg Harbor, New Jersey.

The police found the women a few hundred feet from each other, and the last one was a mere two hundred feet from a sign welcoming visitors to Atlantic City. Casinos were visible from the crime scene. But the town of Egg Harbor and the motels of Route 322 are a long way from any casino luxury. It is a putrid stretch of wood-frame one-story motels catering to the depraved, the addicted, and the lost. A local woman was quoted as saying, "You don't stay here unless you're doing something wrong."

The local cops had no real leads, and the best they could do was try to keep the prostitutes off the streets. They surmised the killer was likely a john, as all four of the women had records for prostitution arrests. Also, a woman named Pam Cavelli had been with three of the four women right before they had vanished and claimed that all four had been fishing for customers.

According to the county coroner, they also had some bad things running around in their blood when they died. Kim Raffo, thirty-five, and Tracy Ann Roberts, twenty-three, had ingested massive amounts of cocaine—enough to render them immobile—before they died. Barbara Breider, forty-two, had heroin in her system, and Molly Dits, twenty, was found to have alcohol in her blood. The police worked with the theory that they had partied with a john who later killed them all.

As the story heated up, the casino management in Atlantic City wanted it to go away. In 1976 New Jersey had voted to allow gambling casinos, to revitalize the area and to give Las Vegas an East Coast run for the gaming buck. In 1978 the first hotel opened. Others were to follow. But the urban renewal never reached past the luxury hotels. Atlantic City and the surrounding areas can be very dangerous places, and tourists are kept protected and herded together. Visitors are encouraged to stay in their hotels to keep the gambling going. No one takes a stroll down the side streets of Atlantic City unless they know the area well.

Around Atlantic City the cops and the prostitutes all agreed on the theory that a john did the killing. The police looked into all the boyfriends, ex-husbands, and pimps of the dead women, and they all came up clean. The case remains unsolved to this day.

•••

From 1978 to 1991 Jeffrey Dahmer killed at least seventeen young men. Dahmer was also a cannibal, cutting up and eating various body parts of his victims. When news of these killings and cannibalism hit the national police blotters, Dahmer may have won the title of the most foul serial killer in American history.

As stated earlier, sometimes luck is what leads to capturing serial killers. And a lot of times bad luck is the last luck of the victims. In

May of 1991, Konerk Sinthasumphone, a fourteen-year-old Laotian, ran out of Dahmer's house screaming. He had been kidnapped and tortured by Dahmer the day before, and he was able to escape when Dahmer had gone out to go to the store.

Sinthasumphone had been drugged by Dahmer and was babbling and naked when two paramedics pulled up and put a blanket on him. When Dahmer returned home, he told the paramedics and the police that Sinthasumphone was nineteen and drunk, and they were having a lover's quarrel. He assured both cops that everything was all right. The two women who had called the cops said they suspected Dahmer was hurting the boy, but the cops chose to listen to Dahmer instead.

As Konerk spoke Laotian and could not be understood by the cops, Dahmer's story seemed plausible. The cops took Dahmer and Sinthasumphone back into Dahmer's apartment. The cops observed that the one-bedroom flat was neat and clean, but there was a nasty and musty smell. Dahmer showed the police photos of a smiling Sinthasumphone in bikini briefs. The kid just sat on the sofa, stunned.

The cops left, but what they missed was the body of Tony Hughes, nineteen, on Dahmer's bed. Dahmer had killed Hughes three days earlier. They also failed to run a background check when Dahmer produced his driver's license as ID. They would have found that Dahmer was on probation on child molestation charges. The cops went back to their car and made jokes on the radio about a male-on-male lover's quarrel.

Sinthasumphone was to be Dahmer's fourteenth victim, and if the cops had been just a little bit more curious about the panicked boy that night, they could have saved him and three others. Later when the story hit the police blotter describing just who Dahmer was, the two cops, John Balcercak and Joseph Gabrish, were fired from the Milwaukee PD. They appealed the case and won their jobs back.

On July 22, 1991 two other Milwaukee cops saw Tracy Edwards walking down a Milwaukee street, dazed and with a pair of handcuffs dangling from one wrist. They asked him what happened, and he told them about a weird dude who tried to hurt him. The cops rolled their eyes, figuring this was some wild gay pickup game gone wrong, but to their credit they did their job—and then they got lucky, if you can call finding a dismembered body part "lucky."

The cops went to the building where Edwards had said he was attacked and knocked on apartment 213. Jeffrey Dahmer opened the door with a serene smile and let them in. Dahmer began by telling one cop that Edwards was a street pickup who had run out of the apartment after stealing some of Dahmer's cash. As he was talking, the other cop began a cursory search of the apartment. The cop opened the refrigerator door and yelled, "There is a f—ing head in the refrigerator!"

The first officer attempted to handcuff Dahmer, who put up a fight. It took both cops to subdue him. It would take an army of investigators to sort out the evil in Dahmer's life after he was arrested.

The city of Milwaukee found that Dahmer had killed at least seventeen men, mostly between 1989 and 1991. Dahmer had also eaten some of his victims. The city was so horrified by Dahmer's crimes that it bought the apartment house where he had lived and killed, and tore it down. A memorial garden was to be built on the site, but as of 2007 it remains a weed-filled lot littered with debris.

Dahmer went to trial in July of 1992 and pled not guilty by reason of insanity. The jury didn't buy it, and he was found guilty of fifteen counts of murder and was sentenced to more than 1,000 years in jail.

Dahmer did not fare well in prison. During a church service an inmate tried to slit his throat, but Dahmer survived with minor wounds. In 1994 he wasn't so lucky when an inmate named Christopher Scarver beat Dahmer and another inmate to death with a broom handle. It was a brutal end to a spectacularly brutal person.

•••

In the winter of 1977 a serial killer emerged in New York. This killer was first known as "The .44 Caliber Killer," owing to the type of gun he used, but when police found an utterly psychotic note after a fourth shooting, this madman became known as "Son of Sam." When that hit the police blotter, it lit up everyone's imagination, because now this maniac had a name, as if he were a character in a movie.

This fiend was born in Brooklyn on June 1, 1953 as an unwanted child. His penniless mother felt she had no choice but to put him up for adoption to a decent couple who wanted the child but were unable to conceive.

The adoptive parents took their son to the Bronx where they tried their best to raise him as a decent middle-class child. It became apparent early on that the child had some serious psychological problems. As a ten-year-old he would hang out his sixth-floor window, telling his mother and father that he wished he were dead. His parents sent him to guidance counselors and social workers, but those usual fixtures of such family dramas did nothing for him.

David Berkowitz's first recorded crime was stabbing a young woman in his Bronx neighborhood in 1975. He stabbed her in the arm, and the wound was not serious. The cops never caught him for that crime. In 1975 and 1976 he began setting small fires all across the North Bronx. He lit mailboxes, cars, shrubs, and garbage cans on fire. He would hide and watch the firemen come and put them out. These small crimes were never enough. In the summer of 1976, Berkowitz took up a .44 caliber Bulldog revolver and began to kill.

Berkowitz took to extreme violence just as the city was at its nadir. His killing spree added to the woes of a seemingly dying metropolis. It was a city that was told—in a famous *Daily News* headline—FORD TO CITY: DROP DEAD. The coffers of the treasury were empty. Crime was rampant, and the city's answer was to lay off cops. Arson became endemic, and with the empty city coffers new firemen couldn't be hired to help the overworked crews. If you were a New Yorker in 1977, you knew murder and mayhem. Not much scared you, because if it did, you would have moved out.

In fact, between 1970 and 1980 the population of New York dropped by 800,000 people. Many left, but not many moved in. New York was not a choice destination in those days. In 1976 when the Son of Sam began shooting, he killed only one person. Other criminals full of passion, jealousy, viciousness, evil, poverty, and anger killed 1,622 people in New York that year. The city's police blotter was one long death toll.

In 1977 Berkowitz killed five people, and the other killers committed 1,557 murders. In those two years, 1976 to 1977, 3,179 other people were murdered in New York City, yet the Son of Sam's six killings made the biggest headlines. Readers couldn't get enough of the story once it broke in the daily papers.

That was because of the absolute randomness of Berkowitz's murders. Everyone knew the stories of muggings, shoot-outs, and drug wars. But for someone to come out of the shadows at night and gun down innocent girls and boys in seemingly "safe" neighborhoods was beyond a New Yorker's ken. In the Big Apple victims are usually killed for a reason, not just randomly picked out by a madman and slaughtered. Usually.

But during that time, even with the FBI reporting over 800,000 crimes nationwide in 1977, New Yorkers' main fear was of a mysterious fiend known as the Son of Sam. Maybe it was because of this unknown murderer's creepy name. Or maybe all those urban legends about the young lovers being killed by the escaped murderer as they necked on a moonless night at the local lover's lane seemed to be coming true.

On July 30, 1976 the front page of the *New York Post* had a story about a shooting in a safe neighborhood in the Bronx known as Pelham Bay. Two young women, Jody Valenti and Donna Lauria, had been shot while they were sitting in a 1974 Cutlass Oldsmobile. They were talking about their night at a New Rochelle disco when a lone gunman snuck up on them and started shooting. He killed Lauria and badly wounded Valenti—she luckily recovered.

It was a wild story, and some cops thought it was a mistaken mob hit. The Pelham Bay neighborhood was no stranger to Mafia shootings. Maybe the longhaired girls had been mistaken for hippie drug dealers working the forbidden zone of a good Italian neighborhood. The only problem with that theory was that when the mob boys hit, everyone dies. There would have been no witnesses left. In this shooting, only one girl died. Because Valenti survived she was able to give the police a good eyewitness sketch of the gunman.

After a day or two all the local dailies dropped the story. There were more than 20,000 murders in America in 1976. Our country had become a killing field. Back in 1976 no one knew that the girls would later come to be immortalized as the Son of Sam's first victims. Poor, dead Donna Lauria was forgotten—but not by her father. He drove around for weeks with a shotgun in his car hunting his daughter's killer. He never did meet up with Berkowitz, but he still swears that if Berkowitz gets out of jail he will kill him.

After Berkowitz's July hit in the Bronx, he went to Queens on October 23, 1976. There he hunted down a man and a woman, the daughter of a New York City detective, on 33rd Avenue in Flushing, Queens. They were in a red Volkswagen. Several rounds were fired into the car, shattering the windows. The woman was able to put the car into gear and escape unharmed. The man suffered a head wound, but later recovered.

Berkowitz later said that after that shooting he went to a White Castle on Northern Boulevard to celebrate with a bunch of belly-bomber burgers. He claimed that after this job he thought that shooting couples in cars would be fun.

A month later—again in Queens—on November 27 Berkowitz asked two girls sitting on a stoop on 262nd Street for directions. Before they could answer he opened fire, hitting both. They survived, although one was paralyzed for life.

Neither of these attacks got much press. The police had not made a connection between the shootings.

That would all change on the cold winter night of January 29, 1977. A young Queens couple went out to Forest Hills on a first date to see a new movie called *Rocky*. Afterwards they stopped for a drink at a local pub and then walked quickly to their car, which was parked on Station Plaza.

They sat in the blue Pontiac Firebird shivering in the bitter five-degree temperature waiting for the car to warm up. As they started to snuggle, Berkowitz opened fire with a .44 caliber gun, killing the woman, Christine Freund.

February 1, 1977 marked the first story in the daily papers that alluded to the fact that all of the previous shootings might be connected. The police now suspected they had a serial killer on their hands.

On March 8, 1977 the now-labeled .44 Caliber Killer (soon to be known as Son of Sam) was the top police blotter story when he shot a college student named Virginia Voskerichian as she walked home from the subway to her apartment in Forest Hills, Queens. As the gunman approached, the only defense she had were her textbooks, with which she covered her face. The bullets tore through her books and her head. The shooting took place two blocks away from the January shooting. Berkowitz was gaining in luck, because there were plenty of cop cars in the area but none near enough to hear the shots or to see anyone running away.

This was a street shooting in a busy neighborhood, and police found that quite a few eyewitnesses had seen two completely different-looking people running from the scene. Two police drawings were published; one looked like Berkowitz, and the other was of a soft-featured person (maybe a woman) in a knit cap.

On March 11, 1977 New York's mayor, Abe Beame, held a press conference at the 112th Precinct, which was a few blocks away from the most recent shooting. He announced that a killer was stalking New Yorkers with a .44 caliber gun, and that an NYPD command force, labeled the Omega task force and manned with more than three hundred cops, had been set up to apprehend the fiend.

On April 17, 1977 at 3:00 a.m. on a Sunday morning, a young couple, Alex Esau and Valentina Suriani, were parked in a Mercury Montego along the lonely service road of the Hutchinson River Parkway in the Pelham Bay section of the Bronx. As the couple hugged and kissed, the .44 Caliber Killer snuck up to the car and shot them through the passenger-side window, killing them both.

He walked away and dropped a letter addressed to NYPD Captain Joe Borelli. The letter read: "I am the 'Son of Sam.' I am the monster Beelzebub—the Chubby Behemoth. . . . I am on a different wavelength—programmed to kill. . . . To stop me you must kill me. I'll be back. I'll be back."

On May 30, 1977 the killer got the writing bug again. David Berkowitz mailed a letter from New Jersey to the *Daily News* addressed to columnist Jimmy Breslin. He was at his home in Forest Hills when it reached the *News*.

Breslin describes receiving Berkowitz's missive: "A secretary called me and read some of this madness to me over the phone. She really didn't even want to read it. Said she was scared of it. It was an eerie letter. Very eerie. I told her to get rid of it and give it to the cops. I've made a conscious effort to not remember what it said. It was a sick letter written by a sick, depraved mind. It was hurled out of the depths of insanity. . . . But I will say he is probably the only serial killer in history that knew how to use a semi-colon."

The letter started out with: "Hello from the gutters of NYC, which are filled with dog manure, vomit, stale wine, urine, and blood." This was reminiscent of Robert DeNiro's character, Travis Bickle, in the 1975 film *Taxi Driver*, who let go with a similar tirade to a politician in his cab.

The letter went on, "JB . . . I want to tell you that I read your column daily and I find it quite informative. Sam's a thirsty lad and he won't let me stop killing until he gets his fill of blood. . . . Here are some names to help you along: 'The Wicked King Wicker,' 'The Duke of Death,' 'The Twenty-Two Disciples of Hell,' 'John "Wheaties"—Rapist and Suffocator of Young Girls.'"

It was signed, "Son of Sam." The return address was "Blood and Family, Darkness and Death, Absolute Depravity."

Breslin said, "It has always fascinated me how they could make such a big deal over these serial killers. I mean, why study them? I find them depressing and dull. They're a depraved, hideous, and grisly lot of men who are not even worth studying. Forget them."

After Berkowitz was arrested, Breslin was tired of the whole case and wanted it to go away.

"You were left with nothing after he was caught. Just this little bug with a mind full of oatmeal. He wrote me a letter after he was in jail awhile and it went something like: 'Dear Jimmy, How are you.' And it was full of clichés like, 'The politicians are using me like a political football.'"

Breslin laughed and said, "The letter was written in a scrawl like a twelve-year-old would write. Completely different from the first one. I guess they gave him his medication in prison and then he was all right."

One of the small pamphlets that Berkowitz wrote in prison was called "SON OF SAMhain: [an ancient Druid name for highest-ranking demon] The Incredible True Story of David Berkowitz." He wrote that he and other cult members were, "sons of Sam . . . sons of Satan!" He claimed that he became heavily involved with the occult and witchcraft in 1975.

"I recall a force that would drive me into the darkened streets. . . . I roamed the streets like an alley cat in the darkness. . . . Thoughts of suicide plagued me constantly. . . . I was so depressed and haunted. . . . I was so wild, mixed up and crazy that I could barely hang on to my sanity. . . . I was overwhelmed with thoughts about dying. . . . Books about witchcraft seemed to pop up all around me. Everywhere I looked there appeared a sign . . . pointing me to Satan. . . . To someone who has never been involved in the occult, this could be hard to understand. . . .The power leading me could not be resisted. . . . I had no defense against the devil."

None of his victims had any defense against his .44 caliber bullets.

All serial killers seem to take extended breaks between their evil deeds. Maybe they are trying to stop. Maybe they just want some good old-fashioned rest and relaxation before they kill again. David Berkowitz also took some breaks.

After Berkowitz's double killing in April of 1977 he laid low. The police worked the case hard and received more than 5,000 tips that had to be checked out. Everyone seemed suspect in New York, and the cops also had to listen to scores of nuts claiming they were the Son of Sam.

All was quiet until June 26, 1977 when Sal Lupo left a Queens disco named Elephas with a pretty girl named Judy Placido. They were getting into a red Cadillac when Berkowitz snuck up and shot Placido three times. The windows exploded and Lupo ran back to the disco to get help. Placido survived.

That shooting did it. The only thing that kept the Son of Sam story off the police blotter that summer was the citywide blackout on July 13. New York went dark and looters went wild. More than 3,000 people were arrested. For those few days, Son of Sam was forgotten. It was quite a summer.

Berkowitz wrote another letter promising New York he would strike again on July 29, 1977. That night the streets of the city were deserted. Cops sat in cars with female dummies hoping to lure the killer into an attack. The night passed with no shooting, which only made things worse. Everyone knew it was coming.

On July 31, 1977 Stacy Moskowitz and Bobby Violante had just had their first date. They had seen *New York, New York*, the

Martin Scorsese film starring Liza Minnelli and Robert DeNiro. They sat in Violante's car on a quiet street in the Gravesend area of Brooklyn. David Berkowitz snuck up on them and shot Moskowitz once in the head and Violante twice in the face. Violante survived, but Moskowitz died a day later.

The Son of Sam had now killed six people.

A mysterious van was spotted near the site of the shooting of Stacy Moskowitz. There has been a rumor that Moskowitz's killing was filmed and has been traded by "snuff film" fanatics for years.

Snuff films were a 1970s rumor of movies that caught actual killings on tape. No credible source for these films has ever stepped forward, nor have any of them ever been found. Law enforcement officials claim no snuff films exist. But still, some swear Berkowitz's crew of Satanists filmed the killing.

According to writer Maury Terry, "It is believed Berkowitz filmed his murders to circulate within the church of Satan. On the night of the Stacy Moskowitz killing, there was a VW van parked across from the murder site under a bright sodium street lamp."

Like many high-profile cases, what finally brought David Berkowitz down was dogged police work and the luck of a simple parking ticket. His car was tagged the night of the Moskowitz killing two blocks from the crime scene. The cops checked every car ticketed near the shooting scene, and a car belonging to a Yonkers, New York, resident stood out.

An NYPD detective called the Yonkers PD to check out a David Berkowitz, who had gotten a parking ticket in Brooklyn the night Stacy Moskowitz was shot. Police dispatcher Wheat Carr answered the phone. She happened to be the daughter of Sam Carr—the man from whom Berkowitz later claimed he got his name, Son of Sam—and lived behind Berkowitz's apartment building. She told the detective that Berkowitz was a whacko and that he owned guns and she suspected him of being the Son of Sam. The daughter of Sam was the best tip the PD had.

The police staked out Berkowitz's car and waited. On August 10, 1977 four NYPD detectives nabbed Berkowitz as he got into his 1970 Ford Galaxy. His .44 caliber gun was in a paper bag next to him. All Berkowitz said was, "You got me. What took you so long?"

Sid Horowitz, a former court officer captain in Queens Supreme Court went out to King County Hospital with a Queens judge to arraign Berkowitz for his Queens shootings.

Horowitz remembered that day: "I am standing there with the judge and Berkowitz comes out with his head down. I remember saying to myself, 'This is it? This is the Son of Sam!'

"I couldn't believe what a little twerp he was. He was a nothing. He just stared straight ahead with this blank look on his face. I left there shaking my head that this meek little nothing like that had gunned down six people."

Now-retired Brooklyn Supreme Court officer J. B. Fitzgerald worked security for all of Berkowitz's court appearances. Fitzgerald smiled at the memory. He and other Brooklyn court officers were exuberant because they thought they were going to make a ton of money in overtime when the case went to trial. It was one of the biggest cases to ever hit Kings County.

Fitzgerald was one of ten officers who escorted Berkowitz down a long hallway on the seventh floor of 360 Adams Street for a pretrial hearing. As they reached the back door of the courtroom, Berkowitz freaked out and broke away from the officers. He tried to throw himself out of the window. His attempt failed, since all the building's windows were covered with steel mesh. The officers wrestled Berkowitz to the ground. He bit one of the officers and then started to foam at the mouth.

Fitzgerald recalled, "So we bring him into the major's office to calm him down. I mean, ten guys are restraining him. One guy on one arm, one guy on the other arm, one guy on a leg—like that. After about fifteen minutes he starts to calm down. We look around the room and it's just Berkowitz and us.

"One officer says, 'Maybe this flake really is a dog. After all, he bit Murphy.' We all laughed and then one by one we start letting go of him and just let him lie there on the couch. I remember an officer lit a cigarette, and another said to open the window because it was getting stuffy in there. I started to laugh 'cause you gotta remember, this nut just tried to throw himself out the window.

"An officer looked out the window and told Berkowitz, 'If you jumped from the seventh floor, you think you'd crack your skull open like an eggshell?' I think Berkowitz started to get scared."

The next day Fitzgerald was assigned to work inside the courtroom and guard the rail between Berkowitz and the victims' families.

"So in walks Berkowitz and he walks up to the defendant's table and he's looking right at me. Then he starts yelling, 'Stacy's a whore! Stacy's a whore!'

"I'm thinking he's talking to me. Then I realized Stacy's mother, Mrs. Moskowitz, was right behind me. The crowd went wild and rushed the bench, yelling they were going to kill him."

The officers rushed Berkowitz out of the courtroom and tried again the next day. Fitzgerald was assigned to watch the victims' families in plain clothes. As soon as Berkowitz came into the courtroom, someone from the Moskowitz family jumped up on a bench and made a dive for Berkowitz. Fitzgerald caught the guy in midair and wrestled him to the ground.

"We got the guy out of the courtroom, but I gave the arrest to another officer. I wanted to get back inside to where the action was. We were all cocky young roosters back then."

While awaiting trial in Brooklyn, Berkowitz received a brutal jailhouse beating from another inmate in the Brooklyn House of Detention, causing his eyes to hemorrhage. Dr. David Klein was called in to work on the injuries. A year before, Dr. Klein had operated on Bobby Violante's eyes, saving his life after Berkowitz had almost shot both of them out of his head.

Klein told the *Sun-Herald* that as he examined Berkowitz he looked at him and said, "I'm your doctor. I operated on one of your victims and now I am going to treat you."

Klein recalled his mixed feelings: "In the back of your mind you want to strangle him. But you have to respect your oath."

Maybe the beating in Brooklyn did some good. On May 8, 1978 David Berkowitz pled guilty to all charges. In June he was sentenced to more than 365 years in prison. But his trouble in jail would not end. In 1979 an inmate stabbed him across the throat, almost killing him. It took fifty-six stitches to save him, but Berkowitz survived.

Berkowitz first came up for parole in 2002. He refused to attend his parole hearing, admitting he deserved to be in jail until his death. In 2004 he was denied parole and in 2008 he will have the same result. Berkowitz will only leave prison in a coffin.

Gary Kauget is a personal injury attorney who lives and works in Brooklyn. He was once a suspect in the Son of Sam killings. Sitting in his law office, he smiled at the long ago memory.

"In 1977 I was a junior in college at Binghamton University. Every weekend I was driving down to the city because I was having this torrid romance with this girl in Brooklyn. I lived in the Bronx then, on Hutchinson River Parkway. In April of 1977 the Son of Sam killed a girl who lived in my building, right outside our building. That was the killing where Berkowitz dropped the letter to the cops warning them."

Kauget looked up at the ceiling in an effort to remember an event that took place almost thirty years ago. "It was frightening because my cousin, a female, also lived in the same building, and was the same age as the girl who was killed. She was out late that night in Manhattan and my grandmother woke up in the middle of the night and had a bad premonition that something terrible had happened to her. She called the apartment my cousin was staying at to make sure she was all right. Then the next day we found out about the murder."

Kauget sighed, "At first I just thought it was just another murder in the Bronx. Then all this Son of Sam stuff came out and I started to freak out. The suspect was supposed to have lived near a highway, which I did, and he supposedly drove an old mustard-colored car. I owned a mustard '67 Catalina. It was a weird case and I started to follow it."

"I started to get scared. When I'd come home from my girlfriend's house in Brooklyn late at night I'd run from my car to my house. And everyone started to get a little crazy. We'd go out at night cruising the streets looking for Son of Sam. Usually we'd just wind up drunk."

Then a forensic sketch drawing (mug shot after arrest) was released on the police blotter and every paper and TV news station published it. The drawing looked a lot like Gary Kauget.

"That drawing was eerie. It was the summer and I was back in New York working part time in Manhattan. I remember riding the train to work and people kept looking up from their newspapers staring at me. I got the paper and looked at it with a friend. He whistled and said, 'Gary, that looks just like you.' And it did. I got scared. I thought some vigilante nut would kill me while I was walking along the street.

"Then a cop car pulled me over by my house. They had me get out of the car and looked to see if I had weapons. They held my ID and made a call to the precinct. They ran a check on my plates and had me wait. I guess they checked that I had been in Binghamton for most of the murders so they let me go.

"Now I'm freaked out. I look like this mug shot. I wanted out of New York. I didn't even want to go back to work because I was tired of being stared at. When they finally caught Berkowitz a few days later I was relieved."

Kauget laughed, "It was a real letdown when I saw what Son of Sam looked like. He was a wimp. Looked nothing like me."

Here Kauget paused and said, "So I wonder, if Berkowitz didn't look a thing like the face in the mug shot, then just who was that guy?"

•••

For all the fear that Berkowitz produced, he may have been just a copycat to an earlier killer.

From 1969 to 1974 the Zodiac Killer held the San Francisco Bay area hostage with fear. He is known to have killed at least five people, and some cops and reporters believe the number to be even higher.

It is believed that the Zodiac first struck on December 20, 1968 in Benicia, California. He snuck up on a couple parked in a car at a local lover's lane and shot them both dead. The police did a haphazard investigation. They had no witnesses and no leads, and the case got cold very fast.

The Zodiac's next killing was on July 4, 1969 just four miles away in a parking lot at a golf course in Vallejo, California. He had a flashlight taped to his 9 mm, which blinded the couple as he shot dead Darlene Ferrin, twenty-two, and seriously wounded Mike Mageau, nineteen. Mageau survived but was unable to give a solid description of the killer.

About half an hour after the shooting an anonymous call came into the Vallejo PD, and a man claimed responsibility for that night's shooting, along with the one in December 1968 in Benicia. The call was traced to a gas station phone three blocks from the headquarters of the Vallejo PD. The crime scene and phone yielded no fingerprints nor any other useful forensic evidence other than spent bullet casings.

It is not known if the Zodiac Killer knew how disorganized police departments were back then, but it did work in his favor. He killed in different towns and cities, and it took those municipalities years to work together to investigate the same killer. By the time the facts came together Zodiac's trail had gone cold.

The Zodiac took to letter writing, much like Son of Sam would do years later. Zodiac sent letters to the San Francisco dailies using a cryptogram that read, "I like killing people because it is so much fun. It is more fun than killing game in the forrest [*sic*]."

In September of 1969 he knifed a couple hanging out on the shores of Lake Berrysea while wearing a black executioner's hood and a bib over his chest with a weird zodiac symbol—a circle with four lines through it. The man survived, but the woman died. The Zodiac wrote on their car, telling the cops he had done it.

A month later he switched locations, moving to San Francisco. The killer hailed a cab and gunned down the driver, Paul Stine, twenty-nine, at the intersection of Mason and Geary. He killed the cabbie with one bullet in the head from a 9 mm gun.

Now it was the Zodiac's turn to get very lucky. A call was made to 911 and the SFPD put out an all points bulletin that the killer was a black man. According to all witnesses, Zodiac was white. The 911 operator had misheard the caller, who clearly stated that a white male had just shot a cab driver.

This was a fatal error as two San Francisco cops, Dan Fouke and Eric Zelms, saw a suspicious white man just two minutes after the shooting but did not question him, as they thought they were looking for a black man. After the truth came out, the cops bravely came forward and gave a solid description of the killer as a thirty-five to forty-year-old stocky white male.

The SFPD assigned two detectives to the case. Bill Armstrong and Dave Toschi would look into more than 2,500 suspects in the killings. Their best lead came when the Zodiac called the Oakland PD, demanding that a local TV show take his phone call to lawyer F. Lee Bailey on the air. The call was set up, but Zodiac never called. Interestingly, Zodiac had said that he would use the name "Sam" when he called. It makes one wonder if David Berkowitz was following this case, and chose to use the same name when he killed seven years later.

The trail for the Zodiac Killer went cold after 1974 when his last letter arrived at the *San Francisco Chronicle*. The recent movie

Zodiac—along with the best-selling book on which it was based—posits that Arthur Leigh Allen was the Zodiac Killer. The SFPD released DNA testing claiming it is almost certain Allen did not commit the killings. Allen died in 1993, and the Zodiac has not been heard from for more than thirty years.

•••

If Berkowitz was not a Zodiac copycat, then Heriberto Seda definitely was. Seda was a young and twisted fool who lived in the rough Brooklyn neighborhood of East New York. By all accounts he was a loner who liked to go to church and read the Bible obsessively. Something must have gone wrong in his mind, because in November of 1989 he wrote a letter to the cops of the 75th Precinct claiming, "This is the Zodiac."

The letter boasted that he would kill twelve people—one for every sign of the Zodiac—and he already had one kill under his belt. The cops looked into the letter and declared it a hoax. But some smart and savvy detectives kept it handy just in case.

On March 8, 1990 Seda struck as the Zodiac. He shot Mario Orozco on a deserted East New York street. Orozco lived and gave a good description of his shooter—a twenty-year-old man dressed all in black. Seda sent another letter, and the cops knew then that this was the loon who had written the first letter.

He struck again on March 29 and May 31. Seda was using low-caliber bullets fired from a zip gun, a crude, improvised handgun. Both his victims survived, but one, Joe Proce, succumbed to his injuries three weeks later in June. Zodiac had his first kill. In June 1990 he shot another man sitting on a park bench, and that man survived.

Zodiac was no killing machine, but he was dangerous. He targeted the poor and destitute in a ghetto neighborhood where no one looks too long in anyone's face. The police had a very sketchy description of a twenty- to thirty-year-old Hispanic male dressed all in black, but had no solid leads. The cops figured something would turn up because they did have eyewitnesses.

The NYPD set up a fifty-man task force and covered a ten-square-block radius around where the shootings had occurred. Seda saw the cops and jumped on a subway to Manhattan. He walked around Central Park until he found a homeless man on a bench and shot him in the chest. He wrote a note to the NYPD saying he knew all the victims' zodiac signs. Seda actually did know the right signs, and no one knows how he figured that out. His Central Park victim, Larry Parham, had told friends that some weirdo had asked his zodiac sign two days before he was shot.

After Parham was shot, New York City freaked. Sales of birthstones plummeted. News stories urged New Yorkers not to tell their zodiac sign to strangers. The NYPD was convinced that this New York killer had read a best-selling book on the West Coast Zodiac and was mirroring his moves. Seda wanted the city to be in fear, and he succeeded. The NYPD worked furiously on this case. But just when the cops were at their strongest, Seda went into hiding. The NYPD kept the task force for another eleven months, but after there were no more shootings it was disbanded.

It wasn't over. Seda came back in August of 1992 with a fury. He tracked down a woman, Patricia Fonti, and shot her twice. To make sure she was dead, he stabbed her one hundred times. The cops kept the news on this one quiet, and they were not sure if it was the same killer. Seda took another break and came back on June 4, 1993. He shot Jim Weber in the buttocks as Weber walked down the street. Weber survived.

The New York Zodiac did his hunting in areas where there were plenty of people. He was lucky that no one got a good look at him. Cops figured he was either very forgettable looking or he was very fortunate. Turns out he was a little of both.

Joe Diacone wasn't so lucky. On July 20, 1993 Seda walked up to him and at close range fired one shot into his neck, killing him.

Diane Ballard was shot on October 2, 1993 and survived. She would be the last victim. Seda killed three and wounded four and went away. The NYPD had no answer for just who this freak was. The only reason he was caught was because a detective in the 75th Precinct had a long memory.

There were no more Zodiac killings. Three years later, there were no solid leads, but the cops were about to get lucky. On June 18, 1996 the NYPD was called to Seda's home. He'd had an argument with his sister and was holding her hostage with a gun. When she ran out to the fire escape to get away, Seda shot her in the leg.

The NYPD had a tense four-hour standoff with Seda, who quoted scripture and told the cops his sister was the whore of Babylon. He surrendered to the cops, and he was brought to the 75th Precinct. There the cops had him write a statement. A sharp-eyed detective saw the handwriting and realized that Seda had written the original 1989 Zodiac letter—complete with the zodiac symbol at the end.

When Seda was confronted with the Zodiac killings, he confessed it all. He felt relieved that finally they would know who he was. In 1998 Seda was found guilty of three counts of first-degree murder and was sentenced to eighty-three years in jail. A few years ago a magazine published an article reporting that he had fallen in love with a jailhouse transvestite and wanted to marry "her." Apparently their zodiac signs are compatible.

•••

During David Berkowitz's reign of terror, the term "serial killer" came into heavy usage. Criminologist Eric Hickey came up with an exhaustive database on the profile of a serial killer. Of known serial killers, 88 percent were male, with 85 percent of the men being Caucasian. The average age of these killers was 28.5. That is all well and good, but while Berkowitz was making headlines another serial killer was out doing his wet work and getting little or no publicity. This lack of publicity continues to this day, and the most prolific serial killer America has ever had is still relatively unknown. And this guy was a black man.

Coral Eugene Watts was born on November 7, 1953 in West Virginia. When he was two years old, his parents divorced, and his mother, a high-school art teacher, took Watts to Inkster, Michigan, and tried to give him a normal life. She knew Coral was not right. He was always fighting, and at fifteen he attacked a neighborhood woman. Later he tried to kill himself by hanging, and unfortunately for his later victims the cord broke and Watts was sent for psychiatric help.

In 1974 after failing as a mechanic, he enrolled at West Michigan University in Kalamazoo, Michigan. His extracurricular subject would be attacking women. His first two victims survived, but his third victim, a nineteen-year-old coed named Gloria Steele, was stabbed thirty-three times and was killed.

Watts was fingered by one of the surviving girls, and cops brought him in for a grueling thirteen-hour interrogation session. Watts held up very well. The cops couldn't pin the murder on him. He hired a lawyer and then committed himself to a mental hospital for a year. When he got out, he got the first of his many deals with prosecutors, copped a plea to one of the assaults, and got a year in jail. The cops were convinced he had murdered Steele, but the prosecutors told them to come and see them when they had enough evidence.

Coral got out of jail and tried to go straight. He married, but his ex-wife later said Coral would leave the marital bed late at night to go wandering the streets. It is not known if Coral killed anyone during that time.

What is known is that in 1979 he stabbed a woman to death outside a dry cleaner in Ferndale, Michigan. This time there was an eyewitness. A man named Joe Foy was outside his house and witnessed the attack. He gave the Ferndale PD a spot-on description of Watts and his car, but he did not get the license plate number. The Ferndale PD was not up to snuff on Coral Watts like the Ann Arbor PD was, and the two departments never communicated. Luckily Joe Foy never forgot Watts's face.

Watts took to attacking coeds in Ann Arbor, Michigan, in 1980, and after three women were stabbed to death, the killer was dubbed the Sunday Morning Slasher. The Ann Arbor PD got a call in November of 1980 that a man in a car was following a woman walking on the street. The woman ducked into a doorway and got away. The cops arrested Coral Watts.

He was grilled for hours, and the cops knew they had their man. They just couldn't prove it. He was followed around the clock and eventually arrested, but the Ann Arbor PD had to let him go due to lack of evidence. Watts knew the gig was up in Ann Arbor, so he moved on to Columbus, Texas—a small town outside of Houston.

The Ann Arbor PD called the Houston PD and told them they suspected that Watts was a killer and he would continue to kill. The Houston PD followed Watts for a time, but he played the role of a hardworking mechanic who went home right after work so they called off the surveillance.

Watts would try to kill again. In 1982 he attacked two Houston women in their home. He thought he had killed one by strangling her, but she snuck out and called the cops. Watts was arrested, and both women survived.

The Houston PD suspected Watts in a series of murders but could prove nothing. Ira Jones, a Houston prosecutor, decided to cut Watts a deal. If he pled guilty to the attacks on the two women who survived, Jones would give him immunity for any murders he confessed to as long as he gave all the details. Jones knew Watts would get sixty years for the assaults and he reckoned that was as good as a life sentence. Watts took the deal and confessed to thirteen killings in the Houston area. He would only talk about the killings for which he had immunity. Watts knew what he was doing,

and he was laying a long-term trap for the prosecutors.
got away with it.

Police in Michigan and Texas were convinced that Watts might have been responsible for more than eighty murders. They swore this was no exaggeration, and if that is true, Coral Watts would be America's most prolific killer.

Watts was sentenced to sixty years, and immediately set out to appeal the ruling. In 1989 Watts let his plot out of the bag and counted on lady luck being on his side. He filed a motion with the Texas Court of Appeals, which ruled that due to a technicality Watts would not have to serve his full sixty-year term. With his good behavior in prison, he was now listed as a nonviolent inmate. He was now looking at a prison release date of May of 2006. He had been eligible for parole six times from 1990 to 2004 and had been turned down, but the clock was ticking. Texas and Michigan authorities knew they had to do something or Coral Watts would be the first self-confessed serial killer in America to be released from prison.

And that is where Joe Foy came in and Watts's run of luck ran out. Foy had seen Watts kill a woman in Ferndale, Michigan, in 1979, and after watching a TV show on Watts's pending release, he called the Michigan prosecutors' office and told them everything he knew.

Watts had stabbed Helen Duetcher twelve times in 1979, and now he would finally stand trial. He was brought from Texas to Michigan for the trial, and Joe Foy's testimony was riveting. It held up as he told the jury that he could never forget the face of evil he saw that night twenty-five years before. Foy had watched in horror as Watts stabbed the woman over and over, and then turned and stared at Foy before driving away in a car. The defense tried to shake Foy, but he was a stellar witness and the jury believed him. On December 7, 2004 Coral Watts was finally convicted of murder and sent to prison with no possibility of parole.

He almost

/ was supposed to be the Summer of Love, but
(that in Ann Arbor, Michigan. Seven years before
an his Michigan murder spree, another savage man
he Co-Ed Killer haunted that town and surrounding
are… than two years.

Mary F.ezar went out for a walk on July 9, 1967. She was wearing a bright orange dress with white polka dots. A local man on a porch saw Flezar talking with a young, clean-cut man driving a sporty blue car. They chatted and the man pulled away. That was the last time she was seen alive. Her body was found in a field three miles from her house. She had been stabbed more than thirty times.

Police did what they could, but there was not much evidence. One detective observed that the body had been moved at least three times after the killing, and he made a note that maybe the killer liked to come back and visit his victims. This smart police thinking would prove valuable later in the investigation, and then almost ruin the case.

Things were quiet for a year, but on July 6, 1968 Joan Schell, twenty, was found dead. She had also been stabbed, and her body was dumped near a hiking trail. The last man she was seen with was a clean-cut college student from Eastern Michigan University named John Collins. The police brought in Collins, and he gave them a plausible alibi. He also said, "I sure hope you catch the guy."

One day he would regret speaking those words. But in 1968 the cops focused on Joan Schell's boyfriend, who was on the lam after going AWOL from the army. They finally caught up with him, but he had been nowhere near Ann Arbor during the killings.

The killer had a busy summer in 1968. Mary Skelton, sixteen, was found beaten and murdered in a lot in Ypsilanti, and Dawn

Benson, thirteen, was found stabbed to death in Ann Arbor on August 15, 1968. The cops now thought that all these killings were connected, and they were even ready to include a few more unsolved killings of young women in the area as being related. That was fine, but they had no solid leads. Every boyfriend of every woman was questioned and questioned again. Nothing.

The three murders in the summer of 1968 stirred up the locals. Vigilante groups roamed the streets looking for a person about whom they had no clues. All they knew was that they wanted no more killings. The residents of Ann Arbor and Ypsilanti wrote endless editorials about the ineffectiveness of the police. Private citizens collected money to bring in a psychic to help solve the murders. Nothing worked, but the police stayed on the case with a dogged determination.

Summer seemed to be this killer's season. He was done killing for that year, but on July 23, 1969 Karen Sue Beineman was found murdered in the woods outside of Ann Arbor. After two years of working this case, the police knew that the killer might come back to visit his victim. The press was not told of the murder. The cops put a dummy where the body had been. They dressed it up to look like the dead woman, and then six cops hid in the brush.

That night there was a fierce summer rainstorm. The cops saw a young, slim man tramping through the woods heading straight for the dummy. They sprang into action and yelled, "Freeze! Police!"

The man did the exact opposite. He banked on luck and got it. He took off into the woods with the six cops chasing him. In the rain and mud, he was able to get away. It was so dark the cops couldn't even get a decent description.

The next day when the papers got hold of this failed attempt, the chief of police was taken to task. When asked why he didn't have more than six men on the stakeout, he countered that had there been more cops the suspect would have seen them and never gotten close to the body.

Then luck came to the aid of the police. A store clerk read about the murder and had a perfect description of a man who was with Beineman the day she was murdered. A sketch was made, and a cop remembered John Collins, whose appearance exactly matched the sketch. Collins was brought in and questioned, and denied all. A search was done of his house, and blood traces were found there that matched up to Beineman's blood type. Collins's hair matched hair fibers found on the victim's panties, and he was arrested for her murder. Further investigations tagged him with seven murders in all, and he went to trial in August of 1970. He was found guilty of all seven murders and was sentenced to a lifetime in jail, where he still resides in 2007.

But the story does not end there. Collins was found guilty of killing Jane Mixer, twenty-three, on March 21, 1969. Besides it not being a summer killing, police were always wary of this case because Mixer's death had a different MO than the others. Mixer was a happy-go-lucky law student at the University of Michigan. The man she was last seen with looked nothing like John Collins. She had been shot twice with a .22 and strangled with a nylon stocking. All the other women had been raped, stabbed, and beaten. Not Mixer. Her killer was chaste.

In 2004 a new crew of Michigan State Police armed with DNA technology started looking back on old cases. Sergeant Eric Schroeder was struck by the Jane Mixer murder. It just didn't seem to fit in with the rest of Collins's murders. Schroeder had lab techs run a DNA test from blood found on Mixer's hand and clothes, which had been preserved. A match came back for Gary Leiterman, now sixty-two and living in Gobles, Michigan.

Schroeder went to question Leiterman, and he denied being involved in any murder. But Leiterman had been working in the Ann Arbor area as a pharmaceutical salesman in March of 1969. With the DNA evidence he was charged with Mixer's murder.

His secrets started to come out. In 2001 he had been arrested for forging prescriptions from a Kalamazoo hospital where he had worked as a nurse. He was allowed to plead guilty to this charge if he went into rehab. He took the deal, but as it was a felony, he also had to give a DNA sample, which led to his 2004 arrest.

After Leiterman was arrested, cops searched his home and found some nasty child pornography on his computer. He had taken photos of a sixteen-year-old girl who appeared to be drunk. She was posed in a fashion similar to how Jane Mixer's body was found.

At the trial a niece of Jane Mixer went to see what her aunt's killer looked like. She went in expecting to see evil. She almost broke out laughing when she saw Gary Leiterman, a fat and balding sixty-two-year-old man. The niece described him as looking like "Elmer Fudd."

Reporters got a kick out of that and labeled Leiterman the Elmer Fudd Killer. The prosecution's case was based on handwriting found at the murder scene, which matched Leiterman's. The DNA was also important, but the cops may have had too much DNA. Some of the samples came back as a match for John Ruelas. Ruelas was from Detroit and was in jail on a separate murder charge. He had been all of four years old when Mixer was killed.

Leiterman's lawyer pounded the jury on the mixup of DNA and the absurdity of a four-year-old committing a murder. The jury chose to believe that Leiterman's DNA match was real, and convicted him of the murder of Jane Mixer.

Leiterman maintains his innocence while serving a life sentence and is appealing his case over the DNA snafu.

•••

Finally, let's revisit the four poor women killed in Atlantic City in November of 2006. The only good thing about this case is that as of the spring of '07, no one else has been murdered.

There have been some leads, but nothing has come from any of them. A local cop recently said, "It is not like the cops won't try to catch this guy, but it has been months now and the story is out of the papers, and believe me the casino owners want it out of the papers. There is quite a lot of crime just outside of Atlantic City, but if no one writes about it or puts it on TV no one will care. These women will be forgotten unless this guy kills again."

In the winter of 2007 the *New York Times*—a paper that usually shuns the typical police blotter stories—ran a column about the case with the title, "Speculation About Foot Fetishist in Killings." According to the *Times* article, the fact that the four women were all barefoot was "a detail as intriguing as it was mystifying."

The *Times* reported that a Web site had speculated that the killer may have a foot fetish. With that information in mind, some locals and hotel managers recalled a Phoenix man who rented a room in a nearby hotel for three weeks earlier in the fall and who had a fascination with prostitutes and women's shoes. He had even offered a working gal a free foot massage. The man was investigated but came up clean.

As of the summer of 2007, no other similar killings had been reported in or around Atlantic City, at least officially. But most serial killers do not stop at four victims. They go on, sometimes killing years apart, until they are caught, killed, or just get too old for it. Maybe this one will just give it up.

CHAPTER 3

animals

ANIMAL STORIES OF ALL KINDS end up on the police blotter, some funny, some crazy, and others downright strange. Cops have a lot more training to deal with people than with animals, but the inevitable animal encounters occur: pet pythons attack apartment dwellers, circus elephants run amok, or someone finds an alligator in the swimming pool.

When I was a child, my father worked for the New York Fire Department. He toiled his whole career in the South Bronx and routinely saw many wild and weird things, so it took a lot to get my father's attention. But on a call one night, he saw something that got everyone's attention.

This was a police blotter first, at least in the South Bronx. My father had worked a hot and muggy twelve-hour July night shift in 1971, with Ladder 27. At 3:00 in the morning his company had taken a call reporting that a huge seven-foot-tall *headless* corpse was lying on a South Bronx side street. In the early '70s, a body on the street was a common occurrence in the Bronx, so no one at the firehouse hurried to answer the call.

The squad drove to the street, and sure enough there it was: A huge, headless dead man left in the shadow of a building. The firemen put in a call to the medical examiner's office and climbed down from the truck to take a closer look. A police car pulled up, but no one was in a rush to examine the dead body. There was a heat wave in New York, and who knows how long that corpse had been festering on the street?

Undaunted, two firefighters and a cop got closer to the body, and my father heard one of them yell out, "That ain't no damn man! *That's an ape.*"

Sure enough, it was. My father walked up and saw the padded ape hands and feet. The head was gone. Cut off clean. At this moment, my father began to feel a little queasy, because down the block was a hot dog and beef rendering plant that had given plenty of free ground beef to the firefighters over the years. The firemen at my father's house figured the ape carcass had fallen off a meat wagon going to the factory. The rendering plant owner denied any knowledge of the ape, but the firehouse never used the factory's meat again.

•••

When humans and animals get together, strange things can happen. The animals respond according to their instincts—they attack or run away. Humans remain unpredictable.

In November of 2006, a three-man fire truck answered a call from a fifty-eight-year-old man in Kingman, Arizona, who had reported a tree fire in front of his house. Hualapai Valley Fire Department spokeswoman Sandy Edwards said, however, that there really was no fire. The man, Jeffery Cullen, really wanted the firemen to get his cat down from the tree. Cullen admitted to the firefighters that he knew they wouldn't respond to a non-fire call. The battalion chief told Cullen they would not get the cat and that he should call animal control. This refusal apparently enraged the cat lover.

"Cullen went back into the house, got a small black revolver, and came outside shooting." Edwards said.

Luckily, Cullen was a poor shot, and no one was injured. The police quickly responded and arrested Cullen, sticking him with felony assault charges. No one followed up on what happened to the cat in the tree.

•••

According to the U.S. Department of Agriculture Wildlife Service, in 2002 the United States had a record 237,766 wildlife "conflicts" between humans and animals, and almost 38 percent of these encounters were in a suburb or a city. Most animal attacks are the garden-variety dog bite, but some involve a beast that might be the deadliest wild animal in America today: the moose.

Most everyone loves a moose. The lumbering body and the huge antlers on the males make for an endearing lug of an animal. That is part of the problem. From baby boomers being fed the friendly image of Bullwinkle, the moose in the classic 1960s cartoon TV show *Rocky and Bullwinkle*, to countless schools having a moose as a mascot, the animal is popular to the point of seeming harmless. So when one stumbles into a town in Alaska or Maine, everyone wants to get a closer look at the usually shy creature. What everyone forgets is that no one told the moose it was loveable. When people get too close or the moose feels like it is in danger, the beast can become a thousand-pound terror: A male moose weighs 1,000 to 1,600 pounds and stands over six feet tall at the shoulder, and can have antlers with a spread of more than six feet. The females weigh an average of 900 pounds. Such size alone is a threat.

In March of 2007, some Alaskan Fish and Game wardens found out just how dangerous a moose can be. A 911 call came into the game warden's office that a bull moose was acting aggressively toward hikers on a path. The moose was wandering in the wilds outside Juneau, Alaska.

The game officers responded to the call in a helicopter. The plan was for them to shoot the moose with a tranquilizer gun, tag it, and then move it deeper into the wilderness. The Fish and Game cops thought it was a routine call. No one told the moose that.

Doug Larsen, a spokesman for the Alaska game wardens, released a statement that the officers in the helicopter hit the moose with one shot from a tranquilizer gun. The mixture in the tranq shot wasn't strong enough to knock the moose out. All it did was make him mad. Really mad. As the helicopter hovered over the moose, the beast charged the whirlybird and was able to reach up and bash in the tail rotor with its antlers. The copter went into a spin and smashed into the ground. The moose was so strong it was able to ground a helicopter. The two wardens were lucky to escape without injury. The moose wasn't so lucky.

"The animal's jaw was nearly severed by the tail rotor," Larsen said. "It is unfortunate, but we had no choice but to euthanize the moose on the scene."

In Alaska the Fish and Game wardens—the "woods cops"—are kept busy with moose calls. The advice the wardens give to humans faced with a moose is to run like hell.

"With a moose, I recommend people get out of there, run. If you stand your ground, they'll nail you," said Larry Lewis, an Alaskan wildlife warden, giving advice after a moose attacked a hiker in November of 2006. Lewis and his fellow officers, however, are the ones who do not have the luxury of running away.

Game wardens try to shoot troublesome moose with a tranquilizer and then move them deeper into the woods. The last decade has seen a 50 percent increase in moose-human "conflicts" in Alaska, largely due to the lack of wolves to keep the moose herd in check and changes in climate that have caused the beasts to head into civilization for food.

Tranquilizing a moose is an expensive proposition—even when the moose doesn't destroy a $450,000 helicopter. One shot of tranquilizer costs $300 to $400. Sometimes to save money the game wardens in Alaska will call in a specialist to deal with a loose moose. He goes by the sobriquet of "moose whisperer."

Rick Sinnott, a biologist with the Alaskan Department of Fish and Game, is the moose whisperer. Instead of shooting the moose, Sinnott sneaks up behind it and lassoes the animal's hind legs. He pulls the rope, causing the animal to fall to the ground. Then he puts a hood over the beast's head and talks to the moose in a calming tone. Sinnott claims that once the hood is on and the moose can't see, it becomes docile. Once the moose is stable, Sinnott and the game officers tie up the moose and hoist it onto a flatbed truck to be taken into the safety of the deep woods.

Sinnott recently told *Lifestyle News* that there are more than 1,000 moose living near the city of Anchorage, Alaska. Anchorage is the state's largest city, with more than 275,000 residents.

"The moose is the most dangerous animal in Alaska because people see them so much and get used to them," Sinnott said.

Sinnott estimates that at least six people are injured by moose every year in Anchorage, and those six usually have to be hospitalized. Sinnott also claims that the Anchorage city cops get more than five hundred calls a year for moose problems.

One time, Sinnott had to calm down a raging bull moose that had attacked a child's swing set. No one was injured, but the moose snagged the swing set with its antlers and dragged the set around the neighborhood. That was a tough one for Sinnott because he and his fellow officers had to remove the swing set before he could get the hood on the moose's head. Somehow, they pulled it off.

Sinnott also had to get a rather fat moose out of a tight squeeze. The chubby moose had come to town and wandered down into a narrow alley. Halfway into the narrowing alleyway, the moose got stuck. Sinnott had to drag the moose out by its hind legs.

Highway patrol cops in the wilds of northeast and northwest America spend a lot of time responding to accidents involving motor vehicles and moose. The moose usually die in such crashes, but a moose can wreck a vehicle, and quite a few of these collisions are fatal to the driver also.

On June 12, 2003 a bull moose traipsed down Highway 95 in northern Idaho. The moose was hit by a truck and killed, and was left on the side of the road. The truck drove off before the state police arrived at the scene.

Before the cops could arrange for removal of the moose carcass, someone else grabbed the body. Fish and Game agents heard rumors that the owner of a resort called Fiest Creek near the Moyie River had picked up the dead moose and was serving it as a lunch special billed as a "shredded beef sandwich."

Fish and Game warden Greg Johnson confiscated one of the sandwiches, but when tested, the meat proved to be beef. Johnson was also armed with a warrant and searched the resort and the owner's home. He found moose meat in the café owner's private freezer. The owner, Cliff Kramer, was arrested and charged with unlawful possession of a big-game animal.

The charges were later dropped, and Cliff Kramer filed a lawsuit against the Fish and Game wardens. He also promised that he would serve the moose meat at a "Moose Festival" at the Fiest Creek resort.

In 2004, a female moose and her calf wandering in the woods outside of Sibbhult, Sweden, found a bounty of fermented apples and chowed down on the rotting fruit. After getting good and drunk, the two beasts headed into town. They crashed through the plate glass window of an old-age home and chased the old folks down the hall. Frantic residents called the police, and the cops were able to get the moose out of the home and back into the woods.

The Sibbhult police figured they were done with the drunken moose, but those big lushes had other plans. The moose went back to the apples and ate more of them, getting even more looped. They stumbled back into town, and the sight of two moose walking with unsteady legs prompted the residents to call the cops again. Before any damage could be done, the cops chased the moose out of town and then hired a local hunter armed with dogs to chase the moose back into the deep woods, far away from the applejack.

Recently the police department of North Sand Point, Idaho, was getting flooded with 911 calls whenever a moose entered the town. The problem wasn't just the moose—it was the tourists chasing the moose in an attempt to get a photo as the animal ambled through town. The moose would get scared, and a few charged. The humans had been lucky that they were able to flee before the moose got to them.

The chief of police, Mark Lockwood, knew it was only a matter of time before a moose turned on a human and stomped him into the ground, a sure death. So Lockwood came up with a police public service advertisement and had posters plastered throughout the town. The poster had a drawing of a moose and the legend, "Bullwinkle is going to stomp somebody."

Lockwood claimed the ad campaign was a success, as no one got stomped by a moose in North Sand Point and the tourists and residents started giving the moose more room when they came to town.

Some moose have no respect. In March of 2006 Louis Hecht was walking to church in Grand Lake, Colorado. Hecht, the former town mayor, had just turned ninety-two the day before, and he was a well-loved man in Grand Lake. As he approached his church on a Sunday morning, the last thing on his mind was a bull moose, but one came charging upon him and knocked him to the ground.

The animal kicked Hecht twice in the legs before other churchgoers were able to scare off the beast and call the Grand Lake police. The cops chased the moose into a cul-de-sac, and a cop opened fire with his handgun and killed the moose. No fussing with tranquilizer guns in Grand Lake.

Hecht was taken to a nearby hospital and was treated for cuts and bruises, and later released. The moose killing in Grand Lake created a small media sensation. Many people felt the cops had gone too far in killing the moose. Ron Velarde, a Department of Wildlife spokesman, had no qualms over the killing: "All indications are that the moose attack was unprovoked. . . . we will not tolerate wildlife aggression towards people."

In 2006 Myong Chin Ra, seventy-one, was on the campus of the University of Alaska in Anchorage. Ra wanted to visit the recreation center for a senior fitness class. As he gingerly walked on an icy sidewalk, a 900-pound bull moose followed him. Before Ra got into the building, the moose attacked and knocked him down into a snowbank. As Ra struggled to crawl away, the moose proceeded to pound his hooves into Ra's body.

The Anchorage PD arrived and took down the moose with a safety net. Ra was rushed to a hospital but died hours later from internal injuries. The moose, however, was given a reprieve and was freed in the wild. This enraged some of the parents of the university's students, and they demanded to know why the moose wasn't killed.

The campus police then began an investigation into some of the students' behavior toward the moose. There were some eyewitness accounts that some students wearing face masks were pelting the moose with snowballs before Ra was attacked. The moose attack on Ra was filmed, but the video did not show any snowballs being thrown, and as the students were wearing masks, no one was ever charged with baiting the moose.

Sometimes even a dead moose can be dangerous. On February 3, 2005 at 2:00 p.m. Amy Walters was taking a biology test at Penn State in central Pennsylvania. As she sat in a study hall room, a moose head on the wall above her fell off its mount, and the antlers banged into Walter's head and knocked her out.

The professor heard the noise and quickly attended to Walters, but he wasn't sure what had knocked Walters out, so he called the campus police. They took Walters to a hospital where she was treated for cuts and trauma to the head. She quickly recovered, but went right to a lawyer's office and commenced a lawsuit for damages, claiming that getting bopped by a moose head caused her loss of enjoyment of life, embarrassment, and humiliation. The campus police held the moose head in a storage locker, as it was potential evidence in a legal case. The case was later settled out of court, but the college would make no official statement on what had become of the moose's head.

•••

A snake is obviously much smaller than a moose, and also much less loved—and just as dangerous, if not more. In Cincinnati, Ohio, on December 15, 2006 a local snake lover, Ted Dres, entered his boa constrictor's cage to feed the thirteen-foot-long reptile. Perhaps the initial contact between man and serpent was friendly and peaceful, but it took a bad turn: A friend who came looking for Dres found him wrapped tightly in the snake's coils and called the sheriff's office.

Police officers managed to wrestle the powerful constrictor off Dres, following advice from an animal protection agency on how to safely unwind such a snake. But it was too late for Ted Dres. He had been suffocated, and was dead at forty-eight.

"People who keep these types of animals as pets should know exactly what they're doing. You're dealing with a creature that is capable of killing," said Andy Mahlman, a spokesman for the Cincinnati Society for the Prevention of Cruelty to Animals.

The snake was held in an animal shelter, and the authorities sought instructions from Dres's family about what they wanted done with the snake. The snake was later sent to a wild game farm.

Some people are aware of just how deadly a snake can be. On October 25, 2006 in Sunbury, Pennsylvania, Terry Jackson, thirty-six, was threatening to kill herself with a hunting knife. Jackson told the Associated Press, "I just wasn't in the right frame of mind that night."

Her neighbors called the cops, and Jackson, who had been on a drug and alcohol binge, sobered up. She raised snakes in her house to sell to laboratories for extra income, and when the police showed up looking to take her into custody, Jackson grabbed two western diamondback rattlesnakes from a tank. She held the snakes up like weapons to keep the cops away. Guess what? It worked.

But the snakes, being snakes, didn't take sides and turned their fangs on their owner. Jackson shrieked as the rattlers chomped into her arms. The cops made their move and took her down with a stun gun. Animal control agents were able to corral the snakes, and they were later donated to a zoo in Hershey, Pennsylvania.

Jackson was treated for the snake bites at a nearby hospital and recovered. She was arrested and was charged with resisting arrest and reckless endangerment. In March of 2007 she pled guilty to one count of reckless endangerment and received six months house arrest and two years probation, along with mandatory drug and alcohol counseling. Jackson apologized to the cops in the courthouse and said she had wanted to commit suicide that night due to family and substance-abuse problems. So far Jackson has kept her commitment to the court, but no word was forthcoming on whether she planned to raise any more snakes.

A forty-year-old man in Leoben, Austria, was not as lucky as Jackson. The man got good and drunk and then text messaged his girlfriend that he was going to commit suicide. She called the local cops and told them of his plan. When the cops showed up at the man's door, he was holding two sizeable cobras in his hands and told the cops he would let the snakes bite him to death.

The cops ordered the man to put the snakes down as they moved closer to him. The man—who, in keeping with Austrian law, remained nameless on the police blotter—swung the snakes at the cops. He missed, but the cops were seriously freaked out by the swinging cobras.

Then one of the cobras bit into the drunken fool, and one of the cops shot him in the leg. The man dropped the snakes and fell to the floor, screaming in pain. The cops took the man to a local hospital where he lay in critical condition from the combination of snakebite and gunshot wound.

The Austrian had more than sixty snakes living in his apartment. The serpents were taken to a local zoo until homes could be found for them. Somehow, the cast-iron Austrian man recovered (think *you* can take a bullet and a cobra bite simultaneously, tough guy?), and the police charged him with a felony assault.

On April 25, 2007 in Glendale, Arizona, Joseph E. Beadle made the police blotter with a snake story. Beadle, forty, was arrested by the Glendale PD after he coated a three-week-old puppy in olive oil and then fed it to his eight-foot boa constrictor. Cops nabbed Beadle on animal cruelty charges, but to make matters worse, when he appeared in court, it came out that Beadle had let two fifteen-year-old neighborhood boys watch the snake eat the puppy. The boys told the DA's office that they could hear the puppy's bones breaking as the snake squeezed it to death.

The judge lashed into Beadle, calling him a depraved individual. Beadle was freed on $5,000 bail, but he was ordered to undergo drug and psychological counseling. Beadle later pled guilty to one count of animal cruelty—a felony—and was to appear in court on May 29, 2007 for sentencing. He faced up to one year in jail and $150,000 in fines. When Beadle failed to appear in court on May 29, the judge ordered a bench warrant for his arrest. Beadle's lawyer claimed he had no idea where Beadle was, and as of the writing of this book, he remains at large.

The snake that was taken from Beadle's house is now in the care of the Arizona Herpetological Society. The snake will not be destroyed, as officials claim that the snake—along with the puppy—was the victim of Beadle's cruelty.

•••

On a lazy Sunday morning in January of 2007, a three-year-old black bear wandered down from the South Mountain Preserve into the sleepy suburban town of Maplewood, New Jersey. Maplewood prides itself on being a diverse community of 24,000 strivers, and a bear is a rare sight in this upscale suburban town about twenty miles outside of New York City.

Two local cops in a patrol car were startled when they saw the bruin rooting through the trash bin outside the town's train station. The cops called in their bear sighting, and the dispatcher told them to follow it while he called animal control. The bear walked through town with the cop car inching along behind it, turning left or right when the bear turned. Easy enough—the streets were mostly empty—but who knew who might be out early to walk their dog?

"The bear was acting suspicious, like it was afraid of us following him. I think we were more scared of him," one of the Maplewood cops said.

The bear wandered away from the center of town down a street lined with wood-frame homes. A sixty-year-old woman was up brewing coffee, and when she looked out her kitchen window, she saw a black bear staring back at her. She let out a piercing scream, and that was it for the bear. He headed to the nearest and tallest maple tree and climbed to the top.

The cops pulled over and waited by the tree. They called in the location, and soon animal control showed up. Then the Maplewood fire department helped animal control set up a huge net under the maple as curious residents began to line the street. The net was four feet high and as strong as steel, and seemed to be enough cushion for the four-foot-tall bear, which weighed an estimated 250 pounds. When all was ready, an animal control officer stepped up with a tranquilizer gun and fired a dart right into the bruin's ample rump. As the drug took effect, the bear swayed for a minute and then fell out of the tree and onto the net. He was out cold.

The cops helped the animal control workers carry the bear to a makeshift cage on a truck, and a wildlife official made a statement explaining that the bear was going to be examined and brought back to the preserve. He lectured the reporters on how bears don't really hibernate the whole winter. They get up and move around occasionally. But he allowed that this bear had wandered farther than most do in the winter.

•••

In September of 2006, a local police report in the Florida Keys mentioned a forty-two-year-old man who was spearfishing in local waters. While standing in a boat, he shot and hit a goliath grouper—the largest member of the sea bass family, which can weigh more than 250 pounds. What happened next, no fisherman would have been ready for.

"It looks like the fish wrapped the line attached to the spear around the victim's wrist," Monroe County Sheriff Detective Mark Coleman said in a news release. "The fish then went into a hole in a coral rock, effectively pinning the man to the bottom of the ocean."

A local diver saw the man spear the grouper and then get pulled overboard. He dove down to the ocean floor and cut the man loose from his line. But the diver was too late, and when the police met him at the dock, the spear fisherman was dead from drowning.

•••

In the summer of 2006, cops and environmentalists started warning residents up and down the California coast to beware of sea lions. Two sea lions had attacked some tourists, and officials worried that the sea lions at San Francisco's Fisherman's Wharf would turn the tables on the local humans.

In the first incident, a sea lion took a chunk out of a man's leg on the beach at Malibu. In San Francisco a woman from Berkeley was also bitten. Both survived, but with a new respect for nature.

"People should understand these animals are out there not to attack people or humans. But they are out there to survive for themselves," warned Jim Oswald, a spokesman for the Marine Mammal Center in Golden Gate Park.

The sea lions weren't done. In November of 2006 a sea lion went wild in San Francisco's Aquatic Park Lagoon. The rogue sea lion bit fourteen people in one day and chased all of the swimmers out of the water. One woman was bitten six times. Wildlife officials claimed that it was a male sea lion protecting its harem.

None of the swimmers were seriously injured, but were urged to get antibiotic shots in case of infection. Some of the residents thought that the National Park Police were not doing enough to protect them. The cops claimed that their beat was on the shore and they were not going to swim out and do battle with a sea lion. Other locals demanded the rogue sea lion be hunted down, but a spokesman for the park police said that in no way would a hunt be allowed as sea lions are a protected species.

San Francisco remained a hotbed of animal blotter stories. Later in the year, two mountain lions were spotted sunning outside the San Francisco train station near Freemont. The SFPD was called, and about ten radio cars responded. The lions took off for the hills. They got away, but if they are smart, they will stay away from the sea lion's lagoon.

•••

Every year in Florida more than 7,000 alligators are killed under that state's nuisance alligator criteria. If an alligator longer than four feet is perceived to be a threat to people or their pets, that gator is going to be hunted down and killed. Man is the real predator, but don't count the gators out yet. Since 1948 there have been eighteen confirmed fatal alligator attacks in Florida. But May of 2006 was a record-breaking month, as three people were killed by alligators in one week.

On May 14, 2006, Annemarie Campbell, twenty-three, from Paris, Tennessee, was attacked by an alligator while snorkeling in Lake George, about fifty miles southeast of Gainesville, Florida. The eleven-foot monster grabbed Campbell by the head and held on to her as she thrashed about in the gator's jaws trying to get free. Her friends onshore saw her in the gator's mouth and called the police. The gator continued to hold the hapless woman underwater in its viselike jaws long enough for the police and fire-rescue officers to free her by poking the gator with sticks. Campbell was rushed to the hospital with massive trauma to her head, and lungs filled with water. There was nothing the doctors could do to save her. The alligator was hunted down the next day by the sheriff's department and shot dead in the lake. The cops ID'd the gator by the scratches near its eyes.

On the same day, 130 miles south of the Campbell attack, Judy Cooper, forty-three, was found dead on the shores of a canal near St. Petersburg. There were no eyewitnesses to the attack, but the police believe that Cooper was struck on the shore. Her right arm was missing, and her shoulder had bite marks consistent with an alligator attack. The sheriff's department hunted down and killed a nine-foot alligator that was found lurking in the canal. The police confirmed that they had gotten the correct beast when Cooper's right arm and hand were found in the gator's belly.

On May 16, 2006 in Fort Lauderdale the local medical examiner said that Yovy Suarez Jimenez, twenty-eight, was attacked and killed by a gator while she was out jogging near a canal. Perhaps her quick movement near water triggered an alligator's aggression, as if she were prey trying to flee. Her dismembered remains were found in the water, and three days later police captured and killed a nine-foot, six-inch alligator that they believed had killed Jimenez. They confirmed that it was the killer gator when they found both of Jimenez's arms in his gut.

Wildlife and law-enforcement authorities were baffled by this rash of deadly attacks. Gators go on the move in the spring as the weather warms and they look for new watery territory and potential mates, which brings them into contact with humans and their pets and can be the harbinger of an attack. But usually gators try to avoid humans, so three fatal alligator attacks so close together was an anomaly.

"As the weather heats up, the alligators' metabolism increases and they have to eat more. They might be moving more, but that shouldn't mean increased alligator attacks," said Willie Puz, the spokesman for the Florida Fish & Wildlife Conservation Commission.

The fatal year in Florida didn't end after the summer. In the early morning darkness on Lake Parker—a known habitat for large and foreboding alligators—on November 29, 2006 Deputy Billy Osborne of the Polk County Sheriff's Department came upon a naked man in the jaws of an alligator.

Osborne had gotten a 911 call from someone saying that he heard a man yelling, "Help, a gator's got me!"

When Deputy Osborne got out of his radio motor patrol car (RMP) and walked near the lake, he could hear someone in the marsh yelling for help. Osborne rushed through the weedy, muddy water until he reached the man held fast in the gator's jaws. Osborne grabbed the man's legs and began to try to pull him away from the big reptile. Two other deputies arrived, came running, and joined in the splashing, muddy fight.

"We were pretty much playing tug of war," Osborne later told a local reporter.

With the three deputies pulling, the alligator gave up the fight and let go of forty-five-year-old Adrian Apgar of Polk City, Florida. When the deputies got him to shore, the badly injured Apgar told his strange tale to the cops.

Apgar had just scored some crack cocaine, and he had gone down to the shore for some privacy. He lit up his pipe and got good and high. A few minutes later while he was lying on the grass, the gator darted out of the water, grabbed him by the arm, and then dragged him into the marshy lake.

Polk was taken to a local hospital where he was treated for severe bite wounds to both of his arms, buttocks, and right thigh. The wounds were significant, but the doctors assured Polk he would survive the attack.

Later in the day a trapper caught a twelve-foot, six-hundred-pound alligator that was believed to have been the one that attacked Apgar. The authorities claimed that the beast would be destroyed later in the day.

The deputies gave Apgar a pass on the crack issue. But the lesson is clear: smoking crack near gator-infested waters is asking for trouble.

Sometimes the tables are turned on alligators. In Tampa, Florida, Benjamin Hodges, thirty-five, was recently arrested in his front yard. His crime? Field-dressing a dead six-foot alligator because he wanted a new belt.

When the Tampa PD nabbed Hodges he told an Associated Press reporter, "I didn't think there was anything illegal about skinning a dead gator."

Hodges told police that he did not kill the alligator. He claimed he had found the dead carcass floating in the shallow waters of the Hillsborough River. Hodges knew a man who made belts at a Tampa flea market, so he figured he'd take the gator home, skin him, and get some fine genuine alligator leather out of the carcass.

The cops charged him with possessing an alligator—a felony in Florida—and he faced sixty days in jail and a $500 fine. Hodges was released on $2,000 bail.

Our last gator story takes place up north in the suburbs of New York City. For years there has been an urban legend that the sewers of New York are filled with alligators. The theory was that people brought back baby alligators from Florida and when they started to grow they would be flushed down the toilet. Some surmised that dank water was natural for an alligator, so maybe some survived and lived in the dirty water. The problem with this is that for six months of the year, New York is too cold for any alligator to survive. But still, the legend persists.

The myth came alive—for a few minutes anyway—when a strange 911 call came in to the Suffolk County PD. The caller claimed that an alligator was sunning itself on a rock near a small pond in Huntington, Long Island. Huntington is a mere thirty miles from New York City, so some wondered if this was a real call. The cops responded, and the AP reported that as Police Officer Vinny O'Shaughnessy approached the two-foot gator, "He wasn't too happy to see us. We were incredulous at first, but then we knew that we had to do something about it."

The cops called animal control, and the gator was bagged and taken to a nearby shelter. The Suffolk PD is still investigating who released the alligator, because it is against the law in New York State to own an alligator.

•••

In October of 2003 Antoine Yates showed up at a Harlem hospital with huge bite marks on his arms and legs. He told doctors that he had been mauled by a pit bull, but the sawbones didn't buy his story. They sussed out that something much bigger than a dog gave Yates such huge bites.

Yates finally admitted that he was keeping a four-hundred-pound Siberian tiger in his Harlem apartment. Most New York apartments are fairly small, so to share one with a four-hundred-pound wild animal is quite a feat. Yates claimed to have fed the tiger, named Ming, three chickens a week, but that didn't seem to be enough for a growing tiger, so Ming went after one of Yates's kittens. Yates tried to intervene between the tiger and the kitten, hence his visit to the hospital.

Inevitably, the cops showed up. But even they had a hard time figuring out what to do. Neighbors had complained to the housing authority about the bad animal smell coming out of the Yates apartment, but housing had never followed up. Now they would have to.

Then the *New York Post* investigated Yates and found out that he had done the same thing in Philadelphia and fled that city after he was charged with reckless endangerment for keeping wild animals in his apartment. Yates was like a modern-day Dr. Doolittle. When questioned by police, he would not say where he had gotten the tiger. He told the *Post*, "I am trying to create a Garden of Eden, something this world lacks."

Garden of Eden, indeed: along with Ming, Yates had a smaller tiger, two bear cubs, a caiman (a relative of the alligator), and two Rottweilers—all in a small apartment. Yates was lucky to have survived. The police spent hours trying to figure out how to handle all these animals, most of which could inflict a horrendous, even lethal bite.

To see what was going on inside the apartment, a police officer rappelled down the side of the building and looked into the window. Ming charged the cop at the window and broke the glass. The cop yelled and pulled away. He called in—with a sense of disbelief—that the NYPD was up against a huge tiger inside the apartment. They knew they needed more than local police to take this tiger down. Local wildlife officials were called, and the cops waited, each hoping he wouldn't be the one to have to go through the door.

Kerry Burke, a city side reporter for the *Daily News*, commented on Yates and his tiger. Burke had grown up in Boston but had made New York City his home for twenty years. He had a wicked South Boston accent, but he was known and respected as a hard-working New York street reporter.

"When you get a story like a tiger in an apartment or an alligator roaming the halls of a housing project, you find that New York is another world. A tiger is found in Harlem and you find the bizarre secrets of the city. Everyone in that apartment building knew that tiger was there but they kept the secret because New York is a wide open world."

The drama at Yates's apartment ended in smiles when the NYPD was joined by a huge force from the Bronx Zoo and animal control. They went in using riot shields to keep the animals back, and the animal control sharpshooters hit the tigers and bears with a tranq gun.

One cop said later that while it was a scary thing going into an apartment to shoot a tiger, it is scarier to go into an apartment that houses an armed man. No cops were injured in the incident, and the NYPD was hailed as having pulled off a very difficult job with care.

Ming was sent to an animal refugee camp in Berlin, Ohio. Yates was arrested but never did any time, and there has been no word if he has begun another zoo inside an apartment.

•••

On Tuesday, February 27, 2007, a Staten Island man, Franklin Picone, had had it with the annoying local wild turkeys that were taking over his neighborhood. Wild turkeys have made a big comeback in New York City, and they can be seen in some of the remote park areas.

Picone was no stranger to the police blotter. He had been arrested in 1993 for using his house as a safe haven for the Colombo crime family. He claimed he had put his life of crime behind him, but then the turkeys came out.

Fifty turkeys had set up their roost in Picone's neighborhood and were driving everyone crazy. Picone broke out some bottle rockets and shot at the turkeys. Most neighbors cheered, but one called the cops. Picone was arrested because turkeys are on the protected species list.

His neighbors defended his actions, claiming they would have shot rockets at the gobblers also. When Picone was led away in cuffs, one neighbor swore he heard the turkeys cackling at the sight of their shooter under arrest.

The neighbor told a reporter that the turkeys made sounds like "laughter," and he wondered if the turkeys were mocking their enemy. Imagine what Picone thought as he walked to the police car in handcuffs. Here he was, a made guy in the 1990s Mafia, lowered to shooting at wild turkeys with fireworks and then having the same turkeys mock him as the cops led him away. Oh, the humanity!

Some residents of Brookline, Massachusetts, would have cheered on Picone. In March of 2006 a flock of wild turkeys on Cleveland Circle attacked six people as they left a movie theater. The cops were called, and the turkeys fled. A police spokesperson explained that the residents of Brookline were to blame, because some of them were feeding the turkeys and the turkeys had learned to expect food when they saw humans. If the humans did not provide food, the turkeys would attack.

The people who had been attacked complained about the lack of response from the Brookline PD, and they were told by the police brass that the cops were handcuffed when it came to wild turkeys. The animals are on the endangered species list, and the police have no power over the fowl.

The truth is that turkeys, chickens, and other fowl make cops feel silly when they get involved in these animal "conflicts." In August of 2004 the cops of the Yuba City PD in California had to deal with one wild chicken.

"It was a different kind of call. We don't train for this. You kind of have to improvise," Yuba City PD Lieutenant Bill Ollar told a local reporter.

A man was driving down Highway 99 when a chicken flew across his windshield and got caught in the car's windshield wipers. The man did not know what to do, so he drove to the Yuba City Police Department and asked the cops to help him get the chicken off his car.

The cops laughed as they saw the bird. One suggested that the man turn the wipers on, but all that did was set off the chicken into a "wing flapping, screeching, frenzy."

A cop put on rubber gloves and freed the fowl. When he tried to grab the chicken, it ran off to the police parking lot. None of the cops wanted to get involved in a chicken chase, so they let the bird prowl the lot. The man drove off after thanking the cops, and the police went back inside to write up the incident. The next day Ollar called animal control, and the chicken was captured. The cops never found out the fate of the fowl.

Cops do not like dealing with birds. There is no upside to a cop-and-bird story—at least not for the cop, and probably not for the bird either. The police can only come out of it looking foolish. Cops know this and avoid any contact—if possible—with birds.

Case in point was an incident in Clearwater, Florida, in the spring of 2007. The man involved asked that his name not be used. He was walking around the city and stopped on a park bench to rest. From the corner of his eye he saw a white egret swoop down toward him. The man ducked, but the egret gave him a hard peck on the head. The man ran off—keeping an eye on the bird—and when he saw a Clearwater PD officer on bike patrol, he reported the incident.

The cop called for an ambulance, but the man refused medical attention. He stopped the bleeding with a handkerchief and was more concerned that the wild egret be stopped.

"What do you want me to do?" demanded the cop. "You want me to hunt down and arrest the bird?"

The man had no answer, and watched as the cop rode off on his bike. He saw the egret on a lamppost looking down and decided to get back to his hotel room before the egret decided to swoop down again.

•••

Another animal cops are loathe to get involved with is the pig. The name alone is used as a slur against cops, and pigs are low to the ground and pretty fast and can make any cop look foolish in a chase.

In 2005 the *Independent* newspaper in Gallup, New Mexico, reported that Officer Victor Rodriguez had just started a four-to-midnight tour when he stopped at a Chevron gas station to fill up his patrol car. As Rodriguez pumped the fuel, he saw two pigs chasing a stray dog in a motel parking lot. The dog got away, but the pigs were lurking on the sidewalk of Highway 66 and Rodriguez knew they could cause a serious car accident if they ran out onto the road.

The pigs had escaped from a local farm and were out looking for action. Rodriguez called animal control for backup and approached the two pigs. The 175-pound porkers fled back to the parking lot as the cop neared. Rodriguez managed to chase the two pigs into an area that was cordoned off by an iron fence. He closed the gate, and now he had two prisoners oinking away. The pigs ate a bush in their new pen and started to bury their snouts in the dirt.

The cop had to guard the pigs for forty-five minutes while he waited for animal control officers to show up. The owner of the pigs arrived, and he and Rodriguez had a good laugh over the pigscapade. The cop asked the farmer what kind of pigs he had here. The farmer laughed and told him, "Pork chops."

The animal control officers finally showed up, and they lassoed the pigs with a sturdy rope. Due to the girth of the pigs, Officer Rodriguez had to help drag the animals to the agency truck. The pigs were brought back to the farm, and the owner got ready for a pork roast.

•••

The rest of America may think of performer Wayne Newton as a punch line to a bad joke, but in his hometown of Las Vegas he is highly respected. In 2003 a female adult wallaby, a relative of the kangaroo, escaped from Newton's jungle-like backyard and took to the streets. Newton keeps a menagerie in his home and was asleep when the wallaby made the breakout. Dozens of 911 calls were made to the Las Vegas PD when neighbors woke up to a wallaby hopping down their busy street.

CBS News reported that Harry Sullard got a call from his son that a kangaroo was out running on his street. Sullard—a self-described redneck rodeo buff—grabbed a lasso from his garage and jumped into his pickup truck to chase down the wallaby, which Newton had named Priscilla.

Sullard, a Vegas PD patrol car, and officers in an animal control car were now tailing the escaped wallaby. Sullard broke out his lasso and threw it at the wallaby from his truck window. He missed the first two times he tossed the rope. The third time was a charm, and Sullard brought the animal down.

The animal control officers calmed the wallaby down, and she was brought right back to Newton's compound. The Vegas PD brought no charges against Wayne Newton, who promised he would look into how the wallaby escaped. It might have helped that Newton is a generous contributor to the Las Vegas PD, but neither the high-pitched singer nor the cops made any comment on that.

•••

In June of 1999 a rodeo company from North Carolina came to Queens, New York, to put on a rodeo for the city slickers. The company set up shop in a parking lot, but before the show could go on, the NYPD showed up and asked the manager for his permit.

The rodeo company had not bothered with permits, so the cops shut it down. The workers were loading nine bulls into a truck when one of the bulls bucked and broke through the barricades.

Detective Robert Samuel told AP, "I guess that bull didn't want to go."

The bull tore through the crowded Queens streets as people screamed and ran to get out of its way. The cops followed in pursuit, as did rodeo workers armed with lassos to corral the bull.

The bull ran five blocks before the cops came up with a plan. One cop car herded the bull from the front toward an empty parking lot as another cop car came up from the rear, aiming the bull in the same direction. The bull had other ideas and would not go gently into the lot. He wanted to see New York.

By this time the NYPD had had enough. A call was made to the higher-ups in the police department, and it was declared that the bull was a menace to the citizens of Queens and had to be put down. There was no time to call animal control or get a tranq gun. The cops' 9 mm guns would suffice. The bull was shot three times and died on the streets of Queens. The rodeo truck came and took the body away, and they were given tickets for having an unlicensed rodeo within the city limits.

●●●

Sometimes an animal can aid cops in catching a criminal. In 1982 Frank McDonald was a newly minted detective for the NYPD and was working in a robbery squad in the 52nd Precinct. The 52nd was a fast-changing neighborhood that was slipping from working class into poverty and crime. McDonald liked the 52nd because it had what he called "good crime."

Good crime to McDonald was to hunt down serial burglars and serious criminals. Bad crime was petty theft and neighborhoods that had little crime. He was a cop's cop and wanted the action. In the 52nd he would get it.

One day on a winter afternoon his squad received a report of a mugging. A nun from Saint Nicholas of Tolentine Church had been mugged in the apartment building where she lived. In the lobby a heavyset Latin man had attacked her and stolen her purse.

McDonald hated bullies, and a man that could mug a woman—not to mention a nun—and punch her in the face wasn't much of a man in McDonald's book.

The case was given high priority because the chief of the Bronx detectives was a devout Catholic who was personal friends with the cardinal. The chief had promised the cardinal that any crimes against the Catholic Church, its clergy, or its members would be taken very seriously. McDonald knew he had to crack this case if he was going to have any credence as a Bronx detective.

A cop in uniform met McDonald in the lobby and filled him in on the case. The nun was unhurt, but was brought to a local hospital for observation. Before McDonald could get started, the uniformed cop smiled at him and told him that the mugger had left something behind—his dog. McDonald grinned as he looked down at the big German shepherd. He checked for a dog tag, but the dog had no ID.

McDonald's partners, John Borris and Tony Martin, came up with a novel idea. They knew McDonald was in good shape and had been a runner for the last decade. They told McDonald they were going to pull a move out of an old *Lassie* movie. They would bring the dog out to the street and let him go with the hope that he would run back to his home.

McDonald liked the idea. Borris brought the dog out, and McDonald got into a runner's stance. They let the dog go and off they went. The dog sped up the street with McDonald hot on his tail. The dog ran out into traffic and almost got hit by a car. The dog turned left, and in the middle of the block it ran into the open door of an apartment building.

McDonald ran into the lobby and heard the dog scratching on a door on the third floor. A chubby Latin woman opened the door and claimed that the dog belonged to her husband. She didn't know where he was, but allowed McDonald to look around. He found the nun's purse in a hall closet and took the woman in for questioning. As he led her out he patted the dog.

At the 52nd Precinct, the woman dummied up, and the detectives couldn't get any information out of her. She was released, and the case frustrated McDonald. He knew where the man lived, but he still had to catch him. Every day the Bronx detectives hit the apartment, but they had no luck. The chief demanded they break the case. They got a tip that the man might be staying with relatives in the East Bronx.

McDonald and Borris were driving down Fordham Road to check on the East Bronx tip when they received a call of a bank robbery in progress only a block away. By the time they arrived, the robbers—four young men in ski masks—had fled, but witnesses pointed out a man who had planned the robbery. McDonald arrested the man, who turned out to be the brains of the operation.

When McDonald returned to the 52nd Precinct, he took the man into an interrogation room. While he was leading the man there, a short, chubby Latin fellow said he needed to talk with Detective McDonald. McDonald told him to take a seat and wait. It took some time, but McDonald got the bank robber mastermind to confess after he was told that the four bank robbers had been arrested and were being brought back to the station.

After two hours, McDonald took a break and saw that the chubby Latin man who wanted to talk with him was still sitting in a chair waiting. McDonald asked him what he wanted, and the man said, "I'm the guy that lost his dog."

McDonald couldn't believe his luck. It was the nun mugger. The chief of detectives was in the 52nd because of the bank robbery, and McDonald let him know that not only had he captured the mastermind of the bank robbery, but he also had the nun mugger under arrest.

The nun mugger gave himself up because he knew any cop crazy enough to run after a dog in the Bronx was not likely ever to give up chasing a man who had mugged a nun. Both of McDonald's arrests led to convictions, and both men were sent to prison.

McDonald had a very nice career in the Bronx after that day. And he claims he owes it all to a German shepherd who he only met once.

•••

This final animal tale reflects the old saw about a man biting a dog. In 1998, James F. Welles wrote a book titled *The Story of Stupidity*. Welles knew his subject well. In 2007, Susanna Duffy reported that Welles and a friend were thrown out of a Syracuse, New York, bar. A K-9 police officer with a dog named Renny took the call and tried to break up the fight. The officer released the dog. Welles grabbed Renny and began to choke the dog, and then bit him on the neck.

"I don't think I bit the dog. I just got into a fight with him. I don't really remember. I was pretty drunk," Welles said to the police.

Welles was arrested for animal cruelty, obstruction of justice, and resisting arrest. He was treated for dog bites and was arraigned in the morning and posted bail. Renny the dog was expected to survive.

CHAPTER 4

it came out of the sky

THERE ARE SOME TYPES OF calls to which police just don't want to respond—mainly because they can't win. One of these is a call for a UFO—an unidentified flying object. If a cop states in his report that he saw a UFO, he gets laughed at by his fellow officers. Then the UFO nuts come out, saying that if a cop saw it, it has to be true. The cops would rather just stay out of UFO blotter calls, but sometimes they can't.

On a cold and clear night on January 5, 2000 in St. Clair County, Illinois, Melvin Knoll went out to check on his miniature golf business. It was around 4:00 a.m., and Knoll wanted to make sure no vagrants were on his property vandalizing it. He got out of his truck, walked around the grounds, and saw that all was clear. The putting greens were clean, and there was no garbage and no tramps hanging around. Satisfied that his business was safe, he went back to his truck. He froze in his tracks when he looked up at the night sky.

Knoll saw a huge triangle in the sky, lit by strange lights. The lights glowed on his golf course and bathed it in an eerie light. As the flying object got closer, Knoll was amazed that there was no sound coming from any engines. He got into his truck and started to drive home, but the triangular object in the sky followed him. He got good and spooked and decided to call the police.

Knoll called the Lebanon PD, and they quickly dispatched an officer in an RMP—a radio mobile patrol car. On the radio, the cop in the patrol car confirmed Knoll's sighting. He put on his lights and sirens and took off after the flying object, which was about 1,000 feet above him. As he barked what he saw into the police radio, a cop from a nearby town, Shiloh, joined in the chase and confirmed that the object above them looked like "a black arrowhead."

Another police officer from Millstadt, Illinois, named Craig Stevens picked up the trail. In Stevens's report he wrote, "I observed a very large flying object coming from a southward direction. The object was flying very low, from 500 to 1,000 feet above, and it was moving very slowly."

Another cop from Lebanon confirmed on the police radio that the object was so damn bright that it looked a little like Japan's flag with the rising sun on the horizon. The cops watched, wondering what it was they were following, as the object took off with a swoosh and went up, up, and away.

The cops filed their reports, and the next day the media made hay out of all the photos that were taken of the object. The cops would not comment on what they saw, but they allowed that they had no idea what it was. The Air Force released a statement that it may have been a weather balloon that was used at a nearby base.

One Lebanon cop who would not let a reporter use his name said, "There is no balloon that I have seen that can take off like a jet. That is nonsense. But if I say I saw a UFO I am labeled a nut so on the record I have no comment."

•••

Cops seeing and getting calls for UFOs is no recent phenomenon. On December 21, 1901 constables Johnson and Clark were on foot patrol in the city of Haworth in West Yorkshire, England. It was a cold and clear night—in the north winter seems to be the best time for UFOs to be spotted, mainly because the night air is so crisp—and the constables were out making sure all the store doors were locked.

As Johnson rattled a bootblack's door, Clark saw a pale green light engulfing them. They looked up and saw a cigar-shaped craft about 100 feet in the sky hovering over them. The cops looked up with their mouths open.

The light was so bright that the town square filled with citizens staring at the object in the sky. After ten minutes the green light disappeared and the object flew away toward the horizon. The cops reported the incident, and everyone went back to sleep. Back then UFOs were not in vogue, and no one knew what it was that they saw, and thought that maybe they didn't want to know.

•••

Sometimes cops are the only people to see the UFOs. Just before dawn on January 27, 1976 in Rosenberg, Texas, four UFOs were spotted by police officer Bobby Slawinski. He was alone when he saw these strange objects in the sky. He wasn't sure what to do, and the four objects weren't going anywhere, so he called for a supervisor and waited.

Sergeant Ernie Watson and officer Gil Steen drove out to Slawinski's location. Slawinski lent them his binoculars, and the cops watched the four objects for ninety minutes as they hovered above Rosenberg's sky. In their report they noted that the objects had very bright red, white, and blue lights on the bottom. The cops never figured out if the flying objects were trying to put on a show for America's 1976 bicentennial with some extraterrestrial patriotism with the old red, white, and blue. After ninety minutes, the object took off with incredible speed and seemed to fly straight up to the stars.

The next day their supervisors questioned the cops. No one else reported seeing the objects in Rosenberg. The three cops each had a good record, and they refused to tell the media that what they saw was a UFO. All they would say was that they had no idea what was up in Rosenberg's sky that night.

•••

It was a cloudless night in Dunellen, New Jersey, on December 20, 1958 when police officers Leroy Arboreen and Bernard Talada were on patrol on Center Street. As they turned the corner, Arboreen screamed, "Look! Look!" as he pointed up to the sky.

Both officers saw a hundred-foot-long object above them. Both agreed it looked like a giant cigar.

In Arboreen's report he wrote, "The object came at us from the west. . . . It came to a complete stop. The shape of the object was distinct. The body of the object was solid bright red and gave off a pulsating red glow. The object hovered a few seconds . . . then went straight up like a shot. We watched it until it completely faded beyond the stars."

The next day's Newark *Star Ledger* ran a headline about the cops spying a flying saucer. Many citizens of Dunellen had also seen the UFO. The cops who worked with Talada and Arboreen teased them about the story. Arboreen took exception with the paper because it claimed that the cops said they saw a UFO.

"They got most of the story right but we did not say we saw a flying saucer, but merely that we saw something that was unusual, odd, and eerie."

•••

Some cop-and-UFO stories are harder to explain away, and sometimes cops don't want to shut up about what they saw.

On April 17, 1966 Deputies Dale Spaur and Wilbur Neff were checking out an abandoned car in Portage County, Ohio. It was 5:00 a.m., and the deputies were out of their patrol car when a light came down from the sky. The deputies stared and saw a huge object hovering a hundred feet above them.

Deputy Spaur ran back to the car and called in to the nearest police station, which was in Ravenna, Ohio. Spaur told a sergeant what he saw, and he was ordered to follow the object.

The craft shot off to the east with the Ohio cops in hot pursuit. They drove down the highway with their light and sirens flashing. As they chased the craft, they called out on the radio. Soon they were joined in the chase by other cops. Traffic coming west halted as drivers stared up at the object in the sky.

Spaur made a turn off the highway, and Neff cursed as they thought they had lost the flying object. But whatever was driving the craft wanted to have some fun. It circled back so the cops could continue chasing it. Neff and Spaur noted in their reports that it was like the UFO was playing a game of cat and mouse with them.

Eight cop cars joined in the chase, which went on for eighty-five miles. Spaur and Neff had to give up near Conway, Pennsylvania, when their car ran out of gas.

Pennsylvania state troopers continued chasing the object for about ten more miles until jets sent from a nearby Air Force base approached. It was as if the object knew the game was up, and before the jets could get there, it shot straight up into the sky and disappeared.

Now, this was a case with scores of cops and eyewitnesses who swore that they had seen a UFO. Major Hector Quintalla—who headed the Air Force's Blue Book Project, which documented UFOs—claimed that what the cops saw was a satellite. When the cops argued with him, he said that what they saw might also have been the planet Venus. When the cops laughed at that explanation, they were ordered by Quintalla to not talk about it. They obeyed, but their police blotter files spoke volumes.

The UFO cop chase story became such a legend that Steven Spielberg used it in his 1977 film *Close Encounters of the Third Kind*.

•••

The next three stories cover some cops who had odd close encounters of the very weird kind.

Val Johnson was working as a deputy sheriff in Marshall County, Minnesota, on August 21, 1979. He was on patrol near the North Dakota border. Around 2:00 a.m. he saw a bright light in a distant field and decided to check it out. He called in to report that he was checking out a plane landing nearby that might be one used by smugglers from Canada.

He drove his RMP—a 1977 Ford LTD—into North Dakota, and as he got closer, the object in the sky flew straight at him. The craft then hovered over Johnson's car and filled it with a bright, burning light.

"I heard glass breaking and saw the inside of the car light up with real bright light. . . . After the light hit I didn't remember a thing," Johnson wrote in his incident report.

Johnson claimed he came to some twenty minutes later. He was groggy and had no idea what had happened. His car had been facing west and was now facing east. He called for an ambulance, and when one arrived, Johnson couldn't explain what had happened. His eyes were burned from the bright light, and he was taken to a nearby hospital. A doctor treated his eyes, which had "mild welder burns."

Johnson recovered, but investigators scratched their heads over the damage to his cop car. One headlight was smashed, and the other was not touched. The clock in the car was fourteen minutes fast and could not be reset. The radio antenna was bent on the top, but only the first three inches of it. The rest was untouched. There were four distinct crack patterns in the windshield on the inside and outside of the glass. A Ford engineer checked out the windshield and said he could not explain how such cracks could occur. Dents and creases on the roof and the trunk of the car were consistent with a collision from above.

Johnson maintained that his car had been damaged by a UFO. Cops and others became suspicious when he refused to take a lie detector test, and Philip Klass—a UFO debunker—investigated Johnson's claim and labeled it a fraud. Klass used as proof the fact that Johnson was a known practical joker. Of course, Klass could not explain how Johnson's eyes were damaged, or answer the question of whether a person would go that far for a joke. Also, the dents on the car and windshield had no solid explanation.

Johnson stuck with his UFO story, and Klass was not able to fully debunk it. Johnson's cop car is now on display in the Marshall County Historical Museum, and the director there allows that the damage to the cop car is very unusual and has to be seen to be believed.

•••

On December 3, 1967 at 2:30 a.m., Sergeant Herbert Schirmer, twenty-two, was on patrol in an RMP in Ashland, Nebraska. He was alone and thought it was just another routine night. Schirmer was about to enter the Weird Cop Hall of Fame.

Schirmer spotted bright red lights in the distance. It looked like a truck had stalled, so he drove toward them to see if he could help. As he approached the intersection of Highways 6 and 63, the red lights shot at him. He now knew it was no truck. It was a floating craft that looked like a forty-foot football and hovered about twenty feet above his car.

Schirmer wrote in his police log, "When I first came upon it, the lights were still. But then I flashed my lights at it and the red lights inside the object started going on and off."

Schirmer recalled that he was frozen in his seat as weird lights went on and off. He heard a siren sound, and then the craft above him pulled up and flew off into the night sky. Schirmer estimated the incident took all of ten minutes, yet according to the clock, almost thirty minutes had passed. He was confused by the loss of time. When he got back to the police station, he made an entry for the night: "Saw a flying saucer at the junction of 6 and 63. Believe it or not!"

The next day Schirmer experienced severe physical problems. He fell ill and had frequent headaches. He had a mysterious red welt on the side of his neck. Word of Schirmer's close encounter reached the Condon Commission operating out of Boulder, Colorado, which was investigating UFO sightings. Schirmer was asked to come out to supply information on what he had seen.

In February of 1968 Schirmer went to Boulder and took part in a regressive style of hypnosis. He was able to recall that on December 3, 1967 he was abducted from his patrol car by aliens in the spacecraft that hovered above him. He described the aliens as four-foot, six-inch, friendly little fellows who hailed from Venus. The aliens addressed him as "the watchman for the town" and had long, narrow faces with a gray pallor. They wore silver uniforms with a snake insignia on the front. They told him that their craft drew power from electrical power lines. They talked with Schirmer telepathically and promised him they would visit him two more times in the near future.

Schirmer returned to Ashland. The chief of police had resigned, so he was given the job. Alas, he took over as chief of police as the story on his abduction hit the police blotter. Schirmer became the laughingstock of Ashland, Nebraska. He would pull a motorist over and give a ticket, and the driver would rip it up and tell him he was a crazy fool for thinking aliens abducted him. The tires on his car were slashed, and a brick was thrown through his windshield. The abuse got so bad that his wife left him. Schirmer resigned as police chief and went into hiding.

He moved to Oregon and worked in private security, but when word of the abduction story reached his bosses, he was fired. He kept a low profile after that, but he never recanted the story. Sergeant Herbert Schirmer of Ashland, Nebraska, is an icon in the UFO alien abduction movement.

•••

On April 24, 1964 Sergeant Lonnie Zamora, thirty-one, was on patrol in Socorro, New Mexico. While he was waiting at an intersection, a Chevy Hot Rod ripped by him at a very fast clip. Zamora took off after the speeding Chevy down Highway 85. At about 5:45 p.m., Zamora was startled by the sound of a huge blast.

"At this time I heard a roar and saw a flame in the sky some distance away," he reported.

Zamora abandoned the car chase and set off toward the explosion. He knew that some small buildings were used to store dynamite down where the blast went off, and he thought there might have been an accident.

Zamora followed the smoke from the explosion, and it led him down a small gravel road. He was within a hundred yards when the smoke cleared. Zamora saw a shiny white object that looked like it might have been an overturned car. He saw two small people wearing white overalls outside the object. When the wee people saw Zamora's car, they jumped and hid behind the object.

Zamora called in on the police radio what he was observing, and then started to walk closer to the object to get a better look. Zamora claimed he heard three loud thumps—like doors being slammed—and then a huge noise. He saw smoke and flames and jumped under a cliff to get protection.

When he looked up, the object was gone, and Zamora could see it flying off into the afternoon sky. Sergeant M. S. Chavez from the New Mexico State Police was the first officer to respond to Zamora's call. Chavez noted in his report that Zamora looked "terrified."

Chavez told Zamora that he looked like he had seen the devil. "Maybe I have," Zamora replied.

Chavez and Zamora scouted the area and noted that where the object had been, bushes and sagebrush were still smoking from being burned and there were huge indentations in the sand.

Zamora and Chavez filed their reports, and every media outlet sent reporters down to Socorro, New Mexico. The FBI got involved and wanted to find out if Zamora was pulling off a hoax. An FBI agent allowed that Zamora was a good cop and did see something very unusual that day. In the report Zamora is described as a sober, industrious, and conscientious officer and not given to flights of fantasy.

The media demanded an answer from the government about what happened in Socorro. The FBI released a report stating that what Zamora saw was a newly developed craft that was flying out of nearby Holloman Air Force Base, and the small men in white coveralls were pilots.

No one bought this story, but as Zamora refused to talk to any reporters, the tale grew in legend. The Socorro UFO incident would not go away.

Lonnie Zamora eventually retired from the Socorro police and took a job managing a small retail store. He refused all interviews and became somewhat of a recluse. Through the years he maintained his silence, but he never refuted his original story. Zamora was last tracked down in 2003, and he was still living in New Mexico and would not speak to any reporters.

•••

When cops get called out for things falling out of the sky, it is not always a UFO. Before the horrors of 9/11 there was a rash of stories on stowaways hiding in airplanes, and some falling out of their hiding places to the towns below. In what seems like another time, the security measures in place pre-9/11 left quite an opening for stowaways.

If the stowaway survived, you had to admire his pluck and guile to risk everything just to get to America. When one didn't make it and wound up dead on a sidewalk, you mourned a world in which people would go to such lengths to get away from poverty and tyranny.

In the winter of 2000 the residents of Long Beach, Long Island, must have thought that some mysterious biblical plague had cursed their small seaside village. Things were falling from the sky and hurtling down toward their beach. What dropped from the heavens was neither frogs nor locusts, but rather Dominican stowaways falling from jet planes.

At 10:00 p.m. on the cool Saturday of February 26, 2000 a woman—who did not want to be identified—took her Labrador retriever out for a walk down Bay Avenue. It was a quiet night, and she entered the parking area of the Long Beach Memorial Hospital so her pooch could go for a run. Looking up at the dark sky, she could see jets flying overhead as they approached JFK airport in Queens six miles away.

A saltwater breeze blew in from Reynolds Channel. The woman walked slowly, looking over the fence at the calm waters, and then followed the Lab toward the hospital. She saw something odd at the eastern end of the lot. At first it looked like a load of laundry, but when her dog started to growl, she went to take a closer look. She could see it was a man's body, so mangled it looked like he had been tortured. She ran into the hospital and called 911.

Long Beach is on a slim peninsula about a half hour outside of New York City. The south end terminates at the Atlantic Ocean and channels border the north side. While it is within the borders of Nassau County, the town has its own police department. But when a murder is involved, the Nassau County Homicide Squad is called in. Any time a body is found on the streets, a homicide is presumed.

The Nassau County cops responded to the parking lot adjacent to the hospital and stared at the body in all its gory wonder. At first they suspected that maybe the man fell from the roof of the hospital. Given that the hospital is only six stories high, such massive trauma seemed unlikely for such a short fall. One cop thought that maybe the body had been dumped—some fiends tortured the man and then dropped him off at a hospital in an ironic twist. But then a Nassau cop remembered that about four years earlier, a man had fallen from a plane a few hundred feet from where this body now lay. That theory started to make sense.

"This guy's body was just gruesome. His leg was twisted up in back of his head and he looked . . . I guess *mangled* is the only way I could put it," an unnamed Nassau cop recalled.

Sergeant William Cocks of Nassau Homicide led the investigation and told a *Newsday* reporter, "No one appears to have seen what happened. . . . If [the victim] jumped off the building he wouldn't have sustained such massive injuries."

The man was scooped up and brought to the Nassau coroner's office. He was a young Hispanic male without any identification. All he had in his pants pockets were British coins and a pack of cigarettes with a stamp from Spain on them. The Nassau County cops became certain that they had a fallen stowaway in their morgue. They contacted the Federal Aviation Administration at Kennedy airport and reported their suspicions. The FAA studied the flight patterns of the night and suggested that the man had been a stowaway in the wheel well of American Airlines Flight 688, a nonstop flight from the Dominican Republic to JFK. The plane landed at 10:00 p.m., so they estimated that the man fell at around 9:45 p.m.

FAA spokesperson Jim Peters denied he had any statistics on how many stowaways die hiding in the wheel wells of jets. His only comment was that, "It's uncommon but not unheard of. Of course we're interested in how this unfortunate individual was able to get on board."

The Nassau cop said, "It happens more than anyone thinks. And I think some of these guys make it through. You either freeze to death up there, suffocate, fall, or you're in America. And I bet a lot of them fall in the water and are pulled out weeks later as floaters and lie around a morgue till someone figures out what to do with them."

He then recalled American Airlines Flight 642 in March of 1996, from which another Dominican descended upon Long Beach. On this warm afternoon, the owner of the Harbor Isle Marina in Hog Island Channel, just across the way from Long Beach Hospital, was out checking on a boat.

He heard a huge explosion in the water and saw that his wooden dock had been soaked by a splash. He thought some kids had set off an M-80, and he went to see what was up. As he moved closer, he saw a man's legs sticking up from the shallow water. He called 911, and Nassau detectives arrived on the scene. As this dead man's body was in relatively good shape, the cops looked at the marina owner like he was crazy when he offered the theory that the man had fallen from the sky.

"I knew he fell out of the sky, and I said it five minutes into this thing, and everyone looked at me like I was nuts," the marina owner reportedly said.

The cops found Dominican pesos in the dead man's pockets. He was wearing maroon jeans with the brand name of Lepesu, which are not sold in America. The police contacted the FAA, and the feds ultimately surmised that a Boeing 767, Flight 642 of American Airlines, which traveled from Puerta Plata in the Dominican Republic to JFK, was this stowaway's last trip.

The Nassau coroner found the man to have a fractured skull and a lacerated liver and heart, but was otherwise "well preserved" for a man who fell 4,000 feet. The coroner assumed that the man might have been alive before he hit the water.

One Nassau cop speculated that "the guy fell asleep, and when the wheel wells opened he just got sucked out. He didn't freeze to death, or the coroner would have seen that, because this guy was found right after he hit. I think some of these guys make it. I heard that out at JFK airport every once in awhile some luggage handler will see a Hispanic guy running for the hills off the tarmac. Once you're on the ground it's easy to avoid customs."

The Nassau cop is right in that it is possible—not likely but still possible—to survive in a plane's wheel well. In 1993 Guillermo Rosales, thirteen, entered a Colombian airport and hid in the wheel well of a cargo plane headed for Miami. He was wearing jeans and a T-shirt. He survived the six and a half hours in the air with very low oxygen and minus-35-degree temperatures at 35,000 feet. Rosales was caught and sent back to Colombia, but by all reports he was none the worse for wear. A grown man with a little more meat on his bones and warmer clothes might easily pull off the same feat.

•••

For years, people have been taking incredible risks hiding in different parts of jets to go places that they had neither the documentation nor money to get into. In 2000, a statistician estimated the odds of two stowaways from the Dominican Republic falling a few hundred feet from each other in Long Beach, Long Island.

He arrived at a conservative estimate of 8-million-to-one odds that these two guys would fall that close to each other. That should have calmed the residents of Long Beach, who looked up into the sky on clear nights and saw a jet coming over the water every few minutes, getting ready to approach JFK airport. But given that New York State's Lotto jackpot odds are 13 million to one, you would have had a better chance of a Dominican dropping on your head in Long Beach than you would at hitting the big Lotto prize.

These stowaways were not just falling on Long Beach. There must have been countless numbers who fell into the ocean, given that any flight out of the Dominican Republic is mostly over water. Every municipality that has a shoreline and pulls in "floaters" every year might have found some. Give the sea a few days to work on a body, and no cause of death may ever be found. If no one claims the body, it goes off to whatever Potter's Field is closest, and that is that.

•••

In 1999 two African teenagers hopped into the wheel well of a flight leaving Africa for Brussels. As the pilot closed the landing gear, the wheels had heated up to over 200 degrees and caused the locked, dark chamber to become an inferno. The teens pulled down their woolen hats over their faces and then passed out. Somewhere along the flight they died. But the bodies weren't discovered until the plane had made four trips on the Africa-Europe circuit. In Brussels, an airline worker saw a skinny leg sticking out of the well. He also found a note with one of the bodies. The poignant missive began with the haunting words, "If we die . . ." The letter touched the heart of most who read it, and Brussels paid for the boys to be returned to Africa inside an airplane, only this time they were riding in coffins. The boys were buried in their homeland, and an unmarked metal marker was placed over their graves.

•••

In 1994 a man stowed away on a plane in Buenos Aires that was heading to Miami. As the wheel wells opened at 3,000 feet, the man fell. He hit the ground on Southwest 42nd Street in Miami and bounced in the air, landing in a man's driveway. Metro-Dade Bureau Sergeant John Mathis said, "All he had on him was a comb, a condom, and the bottom half of a picture." Little more is known about the dead man.

In 1993 a plane approaching the airport near Paris, France, lowered its landing gear, and a man came tumbling out. He landed facedown in a Paris garden as an old woman was planting her perennials. The Paris police wondered if they had a garden killer on their hands and wouldn't believe the story the woman told them about him falling from the sky. But when other witnesses verified her story, the cops looked into airline logs and found the man did fall from a plane.

That same year a Colombian man was found at JFK, frozen to death in the wheel well of a plane from Bogotá, Colombia. Police suspected the dead man was the same Colombian who had been caught twice before in successful stowaways in wheel wells. He depended too much on his luck.

•••

Our last stowaway story made a splash on the police blotter in September of 2003. A twenty-five-year-old man named Charles D. McKinley was working as a shipping clerk at a Bronx, New York, firm called Ameritech. McKinley had been raised outside of Dallas, Texas, in the suburb of DeSoto and became homesick as he worked away in New York. He had some vacation time saved up, but he didn't have the $320 plane fare home.

Then McKinley had an idea. He had been working as a shipping clerk sending computer parts all around America in wooden crates. He figured he could pack himself into one and send himself to his parents' Texas home in a nine-square-foot box. McKinley enlisted the help of a coworker, and on September 5, 2003 he was loaded into a truck and put on a freight plane that took a circuitous fifteen-hour route to Texas.

"I was sitting in the crate thinking, 'Oh, God, someone is going to catch me.' I was looking out between the planks and was waiting for someone to see my eyes and catch me, but no one did," McKinley later reported on his trip.

He wound up on the back of Billy Ray Thomas's delivery truck. Thomas drove to the DeSoto, Texas, home of McKinley's parents to deliver the crate, which was marked "computer parts." When Thomas rang the doorbell, McKinley broke out of the crate with a crowbar he had brought. He shook Thomas's hand and walked into the house.

Apparently there's one thing you don't do in Texas: trick a man into hauling a human being when he thinks he's hauling parts. Thomas, having dragged the five-foot-eight, 170-pound McKinley from the truck to the house, called the police. McKinley was arrested for being a stowaway—a federal misdemeanor—plus some traffic infractions he had ducked out on when he left Texas for New York.

In February of 2004 McKinley was advised by his lawyer to plead guilty because he had admitted to the media that he was guilty of the charge. In the spirit of the crime—which was pretty funny—the judge sentenced McKinley to four months house arrest. McKinley lost his job in New York and tried to make a go of it in Texas. He has kept out of the police blotter since then, so he must be doing something right.

•••

Random people descending from the sky are not just a stowaway phenomenon.

Mike Sergio flew into police-blotter lore when he parachuted into Shea Stadium during Game Six of the 1986 World Series. America watched as Sergio landed on the grass at Shea. He was quickly arrested, but he became a Mets legend because of his stunt. But this was not his first time. Before that he was involved in a stunt in which Owen Quinn became the first man to parachute off the roof of the World Trade Center in 1975.

Sergio is a bear of a man: tall, portly, with long, wavy, silvery gray hair. "I was about a hundred pounds lighter when I made that jump," he noted. "I'll get back to that weight when I start Atkins again. When I'm thin, I think I look a little like Christopher Walken."

Sergio, fifty-six, grew up in Astoria. He talks with a fast New York accent and good humor. Sergio's father owned a waterproofing business and his mother worked part-time at Shea Stadium as an office clerk. Some days Sergio went to work with his mother and was free to roam the stadium—which would come in handy for his 1986 jump. "I got to go all over the place. I knew where all the tunnels led to. I knew Shea inside and out."

Sergio described his interest in skydiving: "When I was a kid, my brothers and I used to watch a TV show called *Ripcord*, which was about parachutists. We loved it, and we used to tie pillowcases on our backs like they were parachutes and we would jump off the banister. When I got older there was this guy in Astoria called Pete the Greek who was going out to New Jersey to take jumping lessons, and I went with him. I loved it from the first time."

At a jumping school Sergio met Owen Quinn, who became his jumping instructor and mentor. Quinn told Sergio his plan to jump off the World Trade Center with a parachute, and asked if he would help with the caper. Sergio signed on, and in July of 1975 his job was to distract the lone security guard so Quinn could reach the roof and prepare. Quinn was arrested when he landed, but Sergio got away clean.

"Owen Quinn is a good man and he never gave me up. The cops knew he had help but he kept his mouth shut. I got caught because NBC ran my photos, and I knew they would trace it back so I gave myself up."

Sergio and Quinn had twelve court appearances before the case was finally dropped. Sergio continued parachuting and went on to work as a musician, cabbie, and construction worker. In 1981 George Steinbrenner had the idea for Sergio's four-man jumping team to land in Yankee Stadium.

"The game was rained out, but that planted the seed. I thought that it would be cool to see someone jump into a game."

It got better for Sergio when his favorite baseball team—the Mets—made it into the World Series, and Queens native Sergio got swept up in the fever.

"During the games in Boston they released a bunch of balloons that had 'Go Sox' on them. I saw that and it went off in my head like a lightbulb. I was going to parachute into Shea during a game. I was up for the challenge. I said to myself, 'If they think that is great, wait until they see what I'm going to do.' After I made the jump one of the local sportscasters said, 'In Boston they send balloons, but in New York we send human sacrifices.'"

When pressed for details of the jump, Sergio said, "Look, I don't ever want anyone else connected to this. It was a stunt I did and got in a lot of trouble for. I won't even say if I jumped out of a plane or if there even was a pilot."

What is known is that in the top of the first with the Mets on the field and the Red Sox at bat, something came floating down from the night sky. When the crowd realized it was a crazy parachutist with a "Let's Go Mets" banner hanging off his chute pack, they went wild.

"I was so focused on the jump all I heard was a roar," Sergio described. "I figured there was a play in progress and I didn't want to interrupt that and hurt the Mets, so I was ready to veer off into the parking lot. Then I realized that they were cheering for me and that play had stopped. The home plate umpire was staring at me with his mouth open. I landed on the first-base line and Ron Darling gave me a high five."

Sergio was quickly arrested, and the Queens district attorney and the feds pressed him for the name of the pilot who took him into the airspace above Shea. Sergio is a standup guy and wouldn't give a name. The DA held him for contempt and threatened him with eighteen months in jail. They went after Sergio full force, and only backed off when Sergio's younger brother, a cop, was diagnosed with cancer and was in his last days. A few weeks before his brother died the charges were dropped.

•••

Owen Quinn had started it all when he enlisted Sergio into helping him jump off the World Trade Center in 1975.

Owen Quinn was born in 1941 into a childhood of poverty in the Bronx. By the time he was a teenager, it seemed likely that he would wind up as just another Bronx juvenile delinquent on the fast track to a life of crime. His first memories are of how it all turned bad.

"My mother got real sick when I was five," he recalled. "She had a long hospitalization. There was no money in our house and my father couldn't take care of the kids—there were three of us. My younger sister and I had to go live in a home for orphaned children up in the North Bronx for four years. After that my mother got better and my father moved us up to 167th Street in Highbridge, and we were all together again. But I was a wayward kid by then, and Highbridge was filled with Old World Irish Catholic families that had eleven and twelve kids, so I had plenty of company when I ran the streets. We were like the Bowery Boys. I knew the street and I knew how to get in trouble."

Quinn is sixty-six now and a happy, retired grandfather living out on the eastern end of Long Island. But in the 1950s he was sick of high school and knew he had to get to work to stay out of trouble.

"I went to two different high schools and I just didn't like school. It wasn't for me. It didn't pay. I was headed for some real trouble, so I knew I had to get out of there and work with my hands."

At fifteen, Quinn went to work at day labor jobs. He caught a break in 1960 when he was nineteen and joined up with the Merchant Marines. That changed Quinn's life.

"I found my niche on the water. I loved it. I sailed around the world twice. I met my wife in 1962 in Keenesberg, New Jersey, after sailing back from India."

In 1964 Quinn went to a local airstrip to go parachuting. "It was just a curiosity; I just wanted to jump out of a plane. When I did it, I loved it. I thought that when I die this is what I want to be doing."

His love of parachuting got interrupted in 1966 when he volunteered for a tour of duty with the Merchant Navy in Vietnam. "We delivered all the ammunition. I volunteered for a second tour and then I was done. I knew if I did one more tour I would be doing that for the rest of my life and I didn't want that." And that is about all you will get out of Quinn on Vietnam.

"My first child was born, so I decided to settle down and just do construction. I went back to work with a pick and shovel as a day laborer." A friend got him a better job with the dock builders' union, and Quinn wound up working on the World Trade Center. "We were putting in these huge caissons that we drove into the bedrock and then put steel into them for the plaza in front of the buildings."

As the complex was slowly constructed, Quinn spied a small-scale model of the development in the lobby of the South Tower. Quinn didn't just see New York's tallest buildings—he saw a 1,200-foot drop with no obstructions.

"I had jumped out of planes lower than 1,200. I studied the model and I said to myself, 'I could jump this.' I went to a bunch of guys on my skydiving team and told them I planned to jump off one of the Twin Towers and asked what they thought. Some thought it could be done; others said it was too dangerous."

Quinn decided to go with the yeas. By the early 1970s he had followed his passion for skydiving and had more than 850 jumps behind him. He had done stunt work on the weekends for air shows, and he had his Jump Master license. For two years he watched and waited as the buildings neared completion.

On July 22, 1975 Quinn and Mike Sergio met in the plaza of the World Trade Center. They dressed like construction workers and hid the parachute in a duffel bag with tools on top. No one stopped them, and they were able to work their way up to the top of the North Tower.

"I planned to jump the North Tower—the one with the antenna on top—because the observation deck was on the other one."

Quinn and Sergio were one floor below the roof when a security guard met them. With some slick talking, Sergio distracted the guard while Quinn sneaked up to the roof and put on his parachute. Sergio met him a few minutes later and pulled out his camera to record the event.

"The roof of the towers had an angle so I had to clear that. I stepped back about fifteen feet and ran fast right to the end. I dove off and cleared the building. It was a rush. As I went down I was laughing all the way. I was in my realm and I knew it would be all right because I had packed the chute."

Quinn flew by windows filled with office workers. They saw him, and then called the police to report that a man had just committed suicide. Quinn knew he had to fall sixty stories before he pulled the cord. He used the phone building across the way as a point of reference. "I opened the chute and the next thing I knew I was floating along looking into the window at a secretary, who saw me and her mouth just dropped open. I turned into the building and used it as a buffer against the river wind and then I landed and the cops were on me like white on snow."

He was brought to a psychiatrist at Elmhurst Hospital and then to another at St. Vincent's. He was judged a sane man and was brought to the precinct to be booked. When he got to the station, scores of journalists rushed Quinn and the arresting officers to get a quote. The police had no idea what to charge him with. They settled on trespassing, disorderly conduct, and reckless endangerment. Over the next twelve months Quinn had nineteen court appearances. Mayor Abe Beame was pressured by the media who loved the stunt and asked the presiding judge to drop the case.

Quinn continued skydiving with teams, and he even did some barnstorming, putting on shows in which he walked out onto the wings of planes. Sixteen years ago, Quinn was injured on the job and was forced into an early retirement. He and his wife moved to the eastern reaches of Long Island to be near their grandchildren. Now the only thrills Quinn seeks are hunting and fishing.

Owen Quinn described his feelings on the 9/11 attack: "The only feeling I had that day was a sadness for all those families who had someone trapped under that rubble. It wasn't about me or the building I jumped off of; it was about the people killed. For a week I walked around in a void. We lost seventeen guys from the dockworkers' union."

Quinn—like everyone else—now just has his memories of the Twin Towers. But those memories are unique. He laughed as he mentioned that he had recently been invited to his granddaughter's school to talk about the jump. He can now look back on it all with a smile.

CHAPTER 5

hot cases, cold cases, and court cases

THINK OF THIS CHAPTER AS a mix of the police scanner and the police file, respectively, the "hot cases" that cops are chasing actively, and the "cold cases" that have sat, unattended, in folders for too long—followed by tales of that place where all cops hope to arrive ultimately: the court, where cops can see their hard work sometimes pay off, and sometimes see things get wildly out of hand.

On March 10, 2003 two veteran NYPD detectives were working on Staten Island, New York, setting up a firearms buy and bust on three thugs involved with the deadly street gang known as the Bloods. The cops, Rodney Andrews, thirty-four, and James Nemorin, thirty-six, were solid police. Both had been on the force for seven years and were good friends. They were big, strong men and knew how to handle themselves. Andrews loved to tease Nemorin for his stylish ways of dressing and liked to call him "The Haitian Sensation." Nemorin had been born in Haiti and lived there until he was twenty-one. He came to America and loved his adopted country and city.

Both men were fathers. Andrews had two children and Nemorin three. They were both proud black men, but they were sick and tired of the easy access gang members had to guns in their community. They were going to do something about it even if it was one gun at a time.

They felt like they had set the sting up right, and pulled up to an abandoned firehouse on Hannah Street. The block was empty and quiet. A closed car wash and car repair shop were the only businesses on the street. The cops sat in a leased Nissan Maxima ready to meet their marks. They had gotten one of the Bloods to sell them a Tech 9 submachine gun for $1,200. They parked and looked around, but were not too worried as they had a backup team behind them parked in a nearby gas station.

The gun seller was Omar Green, nineteen. Andrews had set him up for the buy, but Green was clever and recruited Jessie Jacobus, seventeen, and Ronell Wilson, twenty, to deliver the gun and pick up the money. Green knew Jacobus and especially Wilson were looking to gain street cred with the Bloods. They wanted to earn respect from other gang members. Getting them to sell a gun would be a start. Green was also a little suspicious of the two older men, and figured he would send his underlings out to do his dirty work.

The cops planned to hand over the money and get the Tech 9 in their hands—a good bust—and the backup team would join them in arresting the men as they got out of the car. Then they would go after the gun dealer, Omar Green.

The cops weren't scared of Jacobus and Wilson. They were young street punks, and while an undercover gun buy was always dangerous, the kids they were dealing with seemed like goofballs. They were neither physically imposing nor very smart—the cops made them out to be make-believe tough guys.

Andrews was in the driver's seat, and Nemorin sat next to him. They were at the prearranged street. They assumed their backup team was monitoring them with a listening device—but that was a mistake. The audio equipment was malfunctioning, and the backup team was trying to get it to work.

Wilson and Jacobus were on time for the appointment. They jumped into the backseat and talked about the price of the gun. As Andrews reached for the money, Wilson pulled out a 9 mm handgun and shot him once in the head. As Andrews slumped over on the steering wheel, Nemorin begged for his life. Wilson had realized they were cops, and showed no mercy. He shot Nemorin in the head. Jacobus and Wilson dumped the fatally injured cops on Hannah Street and drove off in the Maxima.

The backup team arrived too late and found the detectives lying on the street—bleeding out from their wounds. They rushed them to a local hospital, where both cops were pronounced dead.

This was a hot case. The NYPD knew who the killers were. Nothing enrages police like one of their own getting killed—never mind two. The cops put their steel-toed boots down and within forty-eight hours all three thugs were under arrest. Wilson was bagged as he grabbed a cab in Red Hook, Brooklyn. Jacobus was busted on a street in Staten Island. Green tried to escape the island by dressing up as a woman and taking the Staten Island ferry into Manhattan. He was arrested when a woman thought he looked suspicious and told a cop on the ferry, "Either that's a guy or the ugliest woman I ever saw."

When Wilson was bagged, the arresting officers found some scrawled rap lyrics in his jacket that he had written bragging about the killings: "You better have that vest and dat Glock. Leave a 45 slug in da back of ya head. Cause I'm getting that bread. Ain't gonna stop to I'm dead."

While Wilson wasn't much of a writer, he was prophetic. Green and Jacobus went to prison with life sentences, but on January 30, 2007 Ronell Wilson—now twenty-four—was the first person in fifty years to be sentenced to death in a federal court in New York. True to his punk image to the end, when the death penalty verdict was read, Wilson turned around and stuck his tongue out at the cops' widows.

The head of the NYPD's Detective Association, Mike Palladino, had called for the death penalty when Wilson first went to trial. After Wilson's sentence was announced, Palladino said, "Ronell Wilson executed two hard-working NYPD detectives who devoted their lives to the citizens of New York. Wilson committed the ultimate crime times two. He deserves the ultimate punishment: the death penalty."

Ronell Wilson now spends his long wait to meet his maker on death row in a federal prison in Terre Haute, Indiana. It is the same prison where Oklahoma City bomber Timothy McVeigh was executed.

Wilson remains close to his punk roots. He was in a prison waiting room for a meeting with his lawyer. His lawyer was late, so Wilson got upset and had a temper tantrum. He broke the tables and chairs and then busted up the Plexiglas windows. He told officers, "I ain't got nothing to lose. I am on death row."

Wilson was brought before a federal magistrate and was told that if he didn't behave he would be put in a solitary lockdown and would not be allowed to come out or to have any visitors. Apparently Wilson had something to lose and has behaved himself since he threw his hissy fit.

While Wilson sits on death row, Detective Palladino, forty-eight, has stayed on with the NYPD and continues to be very popular as the union leader for detectives. He has now been a cop for more than twenty-eight years. He could retire tomorrow and get a nice pension, but he would rather be a cop. It is in his blood. Palladino recently said of Wilson's death penalty verdict, "The bottom line is if anyone deserves the death penalty it is Ronell Wilson. He had the opportunity to walk away but in an effort to gain stardom in the gang world he executed two hard-working, dedicated detectives."

•••

The murder of the two detectives in 2003 brought back memories of Palladino's early cop years. Those were the bad days when New

York—like most large cities in America—was rife with crime. Palladino's career started in 1979, and he worked in a city that was on fire. It didn't improve until the mid 1990s, and cops like Palladino, Andrews, and Nemorin deserve some of the credit. New York in 2007 is one of the safest cities in America. The murder rate in 2006 was under 600. During the l980s and early 1990s, some years topped 2,000 murders.

Palladino was no tough guy and was not physically imposing, but he was a Bronx son who wouldn't back down from a fight and he never liked bullies. He was well liked and respected in the neighborhood, and when he became a cop, he earned the nickname "Mikey the Cop."

In 1982 Palladino was working as an anti-crime cop in the 52nd Precinct in the Bronx. The 52nd was the neighborhood he grew up in. He knew all the streets and most of the bad guys. His career was going well because he was an action guy—a cop who liked to work and make arrests.

In September of 1982 Palladino was dating a neighborhood girl who lived on Jerome Avenue. One September night he and the girl sat in his Trans Am in front of her apartment. Palladino saw two guys breaking into a car.

"If they were just trying to boost a car, I would have gone to a pay phone and called the cops. But I noticed one guy had a gun on him so I knew I had to take police action myself," Palladino recently said.

Palladino flew out of the car and told the men to halt, and that he was police. The men took off down Jerome Avenue, and Palladino ran after them. He caught them four blocks away. Somewhere on their run they had ditched the gun.

He had no backup, so he took the thieves to a local social club and asked the patrons there to hold the men while he went back to retrace his steps in an effort to find the gun. The local yahoos let Palladino down when he went back to the club. The members told him they threw the guys a beating.

"These two had come in a gypsy cab, and when the local guys were tuning them up the driver got out and pulled a gun and got them in the cab and they drove off," Palladino said.

The social club patrons gave Palladino a description of the cab, and he followed it down Jerome Avenue near Yankee Stadium.

"This was before cell phones. I followed them into Manhattan across the 155th Street bridge but they lost me there." Palladino said.

The next night as Palladino was lounging in his girlfriend's apartment a local kid knocked on the door and warned Palladino that two cars full of angry Hispanic men were waiting for him outside. Palladino went out with his service revolver tucked in his pants. He was ready. One of the men he'd grabbed the night before pointed at Palladino, and the two cars drove at him. It was a warm night, and there were a lot of people on the street. The thugs didn't seem to care. One man leaned out of the car window while being held by his belt, and emptied his 9 mm clip at Palladino.

Palladino ducked under a car as the bullets popped around him. He couldn't get off a shot, and just hoped the shooter would miss.

"My training and instincts took over. The shooter had a semi-automatic weapon, which was rare back then on the street. I had a five-shot off-duty .38 caliber handgun. I took cover and just counted the shots. It went like fourteen, fifteen, sixteen, seventeen—I couldn't believe that they wouldn't run out of bullets. I couldn't come out from cover because they just shot up the neighborhood," Palladino said.

The cars drove off, and Palladino was amazed that none of the bullets had hit anybody. Later, detectives investigating the case found fourteen shells on the ground. Now this was a hot case. The NYPD took great offense at one of their own being shot at in an attempted assassination. The men in the cars knew Palladino was a cop and didn't seem to care.

An eyewitness had gotten the license plate number and a good description of the car. The car's description and license were given to every patrol cop and detective in the Bronx and Manhattan. The flip side was that the shooters also had Palladino's license number.

"What came out about this gang was that they had girlfriends working in various police precincts as aides. NYPD ran a check, and someone in the 28th Precinct had run my license plate and gotten all my personal information, my address, and it was not good. I was sat down by a detective who specialized in gang activity and he told me what I was facing. The cops where I lived had to be notified, and they did give my family protection. I played it down because I didn't think they would take it that far, but these were some bad guys," Palladino said.

One reason the gang members never got to Palladino was that the NYPD acted fast. The license plate on the shooter's car came back to a phony address, but two nights later a cop in Washington Heights saw the car outside a local restaurant. The driver was nabbed, and he confessed that he was there, but did not shoot at Palladino. He cut a deal and gave up the whole crew.

The gang was known as the Ball Busters—they were a local crew of Dominicans who were part of the drug-dealing and crime wave that were engulfing the Washington Heights neighborhood. That neighborhood was fast becoming a petri dish for mugging and crack cocaine crews. The northern Manhattan neighborhood had been an Irish and Jewish working class district in 1965. That year there was one murder in the 34th Precinct, which covered Washington Heights. By 1991, that precinct had 119 murders—which is more than some entire cities.

In 1982 the Ball Busters were killers in waiting. All eight were charged with attempted murder on Palladino. Some skipped out of town and some took pleas on lesser charges, but the shooter, Oscar Fernandez, got away clean and fled to the Dominican Republic. It burned everyone up that a guy who would shoot at a cop was free to walk the streets in the DR. Fernandez snuck back to New York a few years later and killed two people in an armed robbery in a bodega in Washington Heights. This time Palladino and the two bodega victims got justice, as Fernandez was sent to prison for life.

Palladino didn't know it at the time, but the brazen attack on a cop by a crew of wild Dominicans from Washington Heights was a harbinger of things to come. That neighborhood would become home to a similar crew known as the Wild Cowboys gang. In 1991 the Wild Cowboys were the focus of one of the biggest homicide investigations in America.

•••

The investigation of the Wild Cowboys crew began when some members of the gang were cut off by a Nissan truck on the West Side Highway. They took great offense at that, so they chased down the car and shot the nineteen-year-old driver dead on the highway. For months that shooting was as cold as a cold case could get. When it broke, all the evidence pointed to a gang of killers that came to be known as the Wild Cowboys.

The Wild Cowboys started in the late 1980s in the Washington Heights section of Manhattan. Two Dominican brothers, Lenny and Nelson Sepulveda, grew up on a block where a crack cocaine crew called "Coke Is It" held court. The young boys were impressed by how much money crack brought in. They started as low-level dealers but left that crew when the NYPD brought down the major players.

The Sepulvedas took what they had learned and started their own crack empire, called the Red Top crew, made up of friends they had grown up with. Washington Heights is near the George Washington Bridge—making it easily accessible to the suburbs of New Jersey—and they had quite a clientele. The brothers expanded their operation into the South Bronx and took over a block near Beekman Avenue and 138th Street, turning it into a drug supermarket.

This was the start of seven years of terror. The NYPD estimated that the Wild Cowboys were responsible for more than a hundred murders. They killed rival drug dealers, crackheads that tried to beat them with short money, witnesses that the cops were trying to work, and innocent hardworking folks caught in the crossfire. Sometimes they killed just to show they could. Four members of the gang once took a man they felt had disrespected them into nearby St. Mary's Park and disemboweled him with switchblades.

On May 19, 1991 David Cargill, nineteen, had come home to his Westchester neighborhood after finishing his sophomore year at the Aeronautical College in Florida. That night he was out at a party with two of his friends, John Raguzzi and Kevin Kryzeminski.

The three high-school buddies had left the party and headed into Manhattan for some late-night action. They drove down in Cargill's Nissan pickup truck. After two hours in the city they headed home, going north on the West Side Highway. A red sedan pulled up next to them and the boys heard the sound of gunshots and the car's glass breaking. Raguzzi turned and saw that Cargill had been shot in the head.

Raguzzi grabbed the wheel of the Nissan and turned the vehicle off at the 158th Street Exit. Raguzzi and Kryzeminski called 911, and Cargill was taken to Harlem Hospital were he was pronounced dead.

Detective Gary Dugan took the call. When he saw the report—"Male/White, 19, DOA at Harlem Hospital"—he knew this was not a run of the mill Washington Heights homicide case. He wondered if the shooting was over a perceived slight on the highway. Florida and California had experienced some highway shootings, but in New York they were almost unheard of.

Dugan brought Raguzzi in for questioning. He thought Raguzzi was hiding something. He was. The kid admitted to Dugan that they were in New York that night looking for prostitutes. Raguzzi said there were too many cops around, so they gave up at 4:00 a.m., He told Dugan that no one had followed them and they had no contact with anyone.

Then he remembered that as Cargill was getting on the highway at 57th Street, they almost had an accident with a red sedan.

Raguzzi wasn't sure, but he thought it might have been the same car that opened fire on them five miles later. The only description Raguzzi could give of the men in the red sedan was that they were dark-skinned and possibly Hispanic.

Dugan brooded that this was as cold a case as he had ever had. He knew Washington Heights and worked the case hard, but came up with nothing. In November of 1991 a confidential informant (CI) gave Dugan his first lead. The CI told Dugan that the word on the street was that Cargill had been killed by crack cocaine dealers from Washington Heights. A dealer had just bought a gun and wanted to test it out. He used Cargill for shooting practice. The only name the CI had for the shooter was a nickname—Platano, Spanish for a sweet banana.

On December 16, 1991, a low-level crack dealer named Anthony Green, seventeen, was slinging his wares in an alley on Beekman Avenue in the forgotten and forlorn South Bronx neighborhood of Mott Haven. Sales were brisk as Green was having a fire sale—he was selling $10 crack vials for $5, and the crackheads came running.

Green was selling Yellow Top crack. The problem was that Beekman Avenue was Red Top territory. The yellow and red color of the plastic stoppers on the vials signified the name of the gang selling the crack. Beekman was strictly Red Top, and Green was about to find out how serious the Red Top crew was.

As he was surrounded by crackheads looking for a bargain, Green never saw the eight hooded men that got out of two cars on Beekman Ave. They came into the alley, and two of the men grabbed Green and held him against the brick wall. They pumped six bullets into his chest. Green fell dead as the other men opened fire on everyone in the alley. For thirty seconds it was screaming mayhem. When it ended, the silence was deafening.

The Red Top crew were breaking all the rules. Not only were they going after the dealers, they were shooting customers. They wanted to send a message out on the streets—Do. Not. Mess. With. Us.

When the smoked cleared in the alley, Anthony Green and three others were dead. Four other people had to be hospitalized with gunshot wounds. The shooters ran to their cars and drove away. The New York tabloids had their lead crime story.

Mark Tebbens took the call in the 40th Precinct. Tebbens was a brave street cop, and at six-foot-six and 250 pounds he was one of the few detectives who had instant respect on the rough and tumble streets of the South Bronx. He knew this was a bad shooting. Dealers and their customers being killed represented a whole new style of warfare. One of his street contacts told him that the shootings were committed by the Red Top crew. They were also known as Lenny's Boys, after the crew's leader, Lenny Sepulveda. The source told Tebbens that the shooter who planned the December 16 attack on Beekman Avenue was the gang's top enforcer. Tebbens was told he went by the street name of Platano.

When word got around to other detectives that Tebbens was looking for Platano, he was told he should hook up with a cop in Manhattan North homicide by the name of Gary Dugan. When Tebbens and Dugan compared notes, they realized they were both going after the same crew. But as high profile as these cases were, the NYPD could not spare any more cops—the city had more than 2,000 murders that year.

Tebbens warned Dugan that this would be a tough case to break, because the Red Top crew was notorious for scaring off witnesses. In 1989 Tebbens had worked a double homicide on Beekman Avenue. In that shooting, two rival dealers had been brutally gunned down by the Red Top crew in broad daylight. Tebbens put together a good case, but one by one his witnesses refused to cooperate. They were being threatened by the Red Top crew. By 1991 the case had fallen apart, and the Bronx DA let the case go off the calendar because they had no one to testify.

To break this case, Tebbens worked on the Beekman Ave. stronghold of the Red Top crew. He used a beat-up van to watch the crack operation. He marveled at how sophisticated the Red Top crew was. They owned the whole block. They had lookouts on the roofs and an elaborate maze of alleys and cellars that the crew used as a shield from the NYPD. Tebbens knew it would not be easy breaking into this crew. There were too many levels of hand-to-hand buys to get anyone big. Tebbens needed to find the main stash of drugs so he could arrest some bigger players, and with a large-weight drug charge they might want to testify instead of spending decades in jail.

Dugan handled the Washington Heights side of the investigation. He worked on the Sepulvedas' habits and gathered intel from neighborhood sources. He talked with a former teacher of Lenny Sepulveda and was told that Lenny and his boys were unruly in school and were nothing but a bunch of "wild cowboys." Dugan knew that to break this case he would need the media, and realized that the moniker "Wild Cowboys" would be a good one for the New York tabloids to use.

During his investigation Dugan caught a break. Platano was in jail for drug-dealing charges. Dugan questioned him there. Platano's real name was Wilfredo De Los Angeles, and he was a short, slight man—not the big, bad killer Dugan had imagined. Dugan told him that the NYPD knew he had killed David Cargill.

"The kid on the highway? That wasn't me, that was Lenny."

For two hours he spilled how he and Lenny Sepulveda were out on May 19, 1991 hitting night clubs and drinking $150 bottles of Cristal. In the club's parking lot, a gang member gave Lenny an AK-47. They left the club in a red Monte Carlo and headed back to Washington Heights. At West 57th they were almost hit by a Nissan pickup truck, and Lenny demanded that Platano catch up with the car. He wanted to see if the AK-47 was working. Platano caught up with the pickup truck, and Lenny opened fire with his new gun, killing Cargill.

Now Dugan and Tebbens knew they were on to something. The problem was that no DA would indict Lenny on only one person's testimony—especially given that Platano was a career criminal and a material witness to a murder. Before they could do anything, Platano was released on bail and went into hiding.

By now the NYPD had done enough intel to determine that this crew was involved in scores of homicides—at least a hundred. Now they needed indictments and good evidence, so an elite task force of assistant district attorneys and detectives was set loose on the Wild Cowboys. The Homicide Investigation Unit (HIU) had Dugan and Tebbens as the lead detectives, and Manhattan and Bronx DAs worked together to bring the Wild Cowboys down.

Tebbens knew the Wild Cowboys needed to be taken off the streets before more innocents died. They were too wild even for the ghettos of New York. The Beekman Ave. crew was raking in more than $30,000 a day in crack sales, and the money was making them very powerful. They felt like they were bulletproof and acted like the cops could never touch them—and for the most part, they were right. They had taken over a whole neighborhood and had all the residents living in fear, and the NYPD couldn't do much to break their power. They knew the cops were watching them, and they were wary—but that was about it. They sold drugs openly, knowing the NYPD was clocking their movements. The Wild Cowboys had gotten away with murder—literally—for years, and they thought they always would.

The unsolved crimes boiled Tebbens's blood. A thirteen-year-old deaf girl playing on Beekman Ave. had annoyed one of Lenny's enforcers because he thought she was making too much noise. To shut her up he dropped a weight down on her from the roof. The girl was permanently disabled. Witnesses told Tebbens that Lenny had punched out his girlfriend on Beekman Ave. and then walked away as she lay unconscious on the street. Low-level dealers told Tebbens that they'd had their fingers broken with bricks when they came up short on money. The Wild Cowboys held target practice on the roofs of Beekman Ave. and would shoot into St. Mary's Park at or near people's legs as they walked by. Tebbens had recorded more than twenty sniper incidents in St. Mary's Park. To him it seemed that this South Bronx neighborhood had sunk into the ways of the old Wild West.

The case against the Wild Cowboys started to build. The HIU learned that in 1991 Lenny had killed three rival drug dealers near St. Mary's Park. He fancied himself as Al Pacino in *Scarface* and set about making the Beekman Ave. crack den his world. In another incident, five Red Top members dragged a rival drug dealer into St. Mary's Park and set him on fire. They watched and laughed as he burned to death. The HIU investigated Stanley Tukes, an enforcer for Lenny, who had killed a man at a New Year's Eve party in 1991 and a week later shot and blinded another man who had witnessed the first shooting.

Full-out war was declared on the Cowboys by the NYPD in August of 1992 when a sixteen-year-old boy who was a police witness was gunned down and killed on Beekman Ave. Everyone involved in the case knew that Lenny Sepulveda had to be taken off the street. Mark Tebbens swore he would bring Lenny in himself.

Tebbens walked down Beekman Ave. and saw Lenny in front of a four-story brick building. As big and tall as Tebbens was, he was easy to spot. Tebbens locked eyes with Lenny, and Lenny ran into the building. Tebbens chased him with his gun drawn and caught up with him on the second-floor landing. Tebbens threw him against the wall, but Lenny—a big and strong young man—fought back. Tebbens was surprised how strong Lenny was, and he knew that if a suspect didn't want to be handcuffed it was tough for one cop to do the job.

Lenny managed to wrangle out of Tebbens's grip and ran to the window. Tebbens grabbed Lenny's jacket, but it ripped off his back. Lenny escaped through the window, walked along a ledge, dropped fifteen feet down into an alley, jumped a fence, and ran away. Tebbens cursed himself for not calling for more backup. He had Lenny in his grasp and couldn't close the deal. He knew Sepulveda would go into hiding and would not surface. Tebbens was right. Lenny went to ground and wasn't seen on the street again.

Finally the cops caught a break. A disgruntled crack dealer walked into the 40th Precinct and told the cops he knew the apartment on Beekman Ave. where Lenny kept his stash. This was the break HIU needed. They got a search warrant, and twenty-four detectives crashed into the apartment and found five hundred vials of crack and a cache of weapons. Three workers were arrested and were facing serious felony charges. They decided to cooperate with HIU in return for leaner sentences.

The case against the Wild Cowboys was building. In 1993 Lenny Sepulveda came out of hiding. He was spotted in a Manhattan courthouse for the arraignment of one of his crew. HIU was called, and the court officers kept on eye on him.

Lenny knew Tebbens and the Bronx cops were looking for him, but he was savvy to how fragmented the NYPD could be and figured he was safe in Manhattan. He figured the Bronx didn't tell Manhattan what they were doing. He had no clue that Dugan and HIU were building a case against him in that borough.

Sepulveda entered the courtroom but was wary when he saw the court officers eyeing him. He slowly got up, and when he hit the hallway, he ran down a staircase. HIU cops were in the building, and the court officers alerted them to where Lenny had run. A detective grabbed him in the stairwell and threw him up against the wall. He knew Lenny had fought off Tebbens, so he made a fist and put a knuckle right on Lenny's crotch, pretending it was a gun, and told him if he made a move he would blow his private parts off.

While being questioned, Sepulveda was stunned at the amount of evidence the cops had against him and his crew. He agreed—along with his brother Nelson—to cooperate with the cops in exchange for a twenty-five-year sentence. Lenny and Nelson Sepulveda spilled the beans on their cohorts, and the HIU prepared an indictment against forty-five defendants covering more than sixty felonies. Lenny and Nelson were such cold killers that the assistant district attorneys knew they could never take the stand. They would be torn apart by the opposing lawyers because of their sordid past. And juries always have a hard time with a killer testifying against others to get a deal for themselves. But Gary Dugan was happy that at least one family—the Cargills—would get to hear their son's killer admit that he took their son's life in open court.

When HIU had a mountain of evidence, they arrested the remaining Wild Cowboys. The New York tabloids ran headlines like, "The Wild Cowboys Are Corralled."

Now that the rugged part of the crew was off the streets, Dugan and Tebbens found witnesses easy to come by. Then one by one those that were arrested turned state's evidence. HIU had more than a hundred witnesses ready to testify at trial. The Wild Cowboys were now in jail and no longer ran the streets.

Only nine Wild Cowboy defendants would not take a deal, and they faced an avalanche of testimony against them. The trial started in 1994 in Judge Snyder's courtroom. Snyder was a tough judge and would not tolerate any nonsense from the crew.

The reason most of the Wild Cowboy crew took pleas was that Judge Snyder had just finished a case on the Gheri Curls, a gang similar to the Wild Cowboys. Snyder hit them each with a prison term of more than a hundred years. They were called "bowling score sentences." Word got out about just how harsh this judge was, and a lot of the Cowboys in jail started to think that taking a plea might not be a bad idea.

Rocco Desantis worked as the court clerk for the trial. When asked about the Wild Cowboy crew, Desantis had a lot to say. "This was a very nasty and tough crew of guys. They thought they could control the courtroom. They didn't know what the word *no* meant. They were used to getting their way on the streets and thought that was the way life was. This crew had to learn that we ran the courtroom, not them. We stayed on them from day one.

"Security was very good during the trial. We had over twenty court officers in the courtroom to control the defendants. They learned to respect the court, and during the nine-month trial we had no outbursts."

Desantis was impressed by the intelligence of the Sepulvedas. "Those two brothers could have been CEOs of a major Fortune 500 company. They were that smart. But they took to the streets and decided that murder and drug sales would pay. It did for awhile. They had mansions in the Dominican Republic. But they lost it all."

The Wild Cowboys would have one last stand. During the trial they hired a man from the Dominican Republic to come to New York and do some wet work—he was a hired assassin. The Wild Cowboys had put a death bounty of $25,000 on Judge Snyder and a $10,000 price on Detective Tebbens. Luckily the FBI caught wind of the hit contract, and the man was arrested before he could get near the judge or the cop.

When the trial was over, the jury took more than two weeks to reach a decision, but in the end all nine Wild Cowboys were found guilty and were given sentences ranging from 20 to 158 years. Scores of homicide cases were closed, and the Cargill family got to hear firsthand how Lenny gunned down their son in 1991.

In 2007 all the Wild Cowboys remained in jail. Judge Snyder retired from the bench and ran for district attorney in Manhattan. She lost and now works as a consultant. Detective Gary Dugan has retired, but Detective Mike Tebbens has stayed on working cold cases in the 50th Precinct in the Bronx.

Tebbens is currently investigating a ten-year-old case of a woman who was raped and killed in the Bronx. Tebbens has been at this one for a few years and has recently reported that he has no new leads on the killer, but after the Wild Cowboy case he knows not to ever give up on a case.

•••

Most police departments now have cold case squads. They are becoming legend, with TV shows and movies based on these specialty squads. One case no one has ever solved is what became of the missing money in a long-ago but ever-sensational kidnapping and murder case: the case of the Lindbergh baby.

The case started on March 1, 1932 at around 9:00 p.m. when a twenty-month-old baby, Charles Augustus Lindbergh Jr., was snatched from his crib in Hopewell, New Jersey. The baby was the son of "America's Hero" Charles A. Lindbergh—the man who made aviation history in 1927 when he flew the first solo, nonstop transatlantic flight. He took off alone in a small plane from Long Island and some thirty-six hours later landed in France, and the lanky young man was cheered as the prince of the sky. He and his wife, writer Anne Morrow Lindbergh, were the country's darlings, and when they had their first baby in 1930, everyone wanted to get a look at the blessed progeny. The "fat lamb," as his mother called him, was a cute towheaded toddler.

The child was discovered missing by the baby's nurse, Betty Gow, an hour after he was snatched. She ran and told the Lindberghs, who were home. They called the Hopewell Police, who knew this was a big deal and brought in the New Jersey State Police.

The same night the baby went missing, the Lindberghs found a ransom note on the windowsill of the nursery demanding $50,000 dollars and the Lindberghs' silence in exchange for the safe return of their child. In 1932—the height of the Depression—unemployment was at 25 percent, and kidnapping the rich had become a trendy crime. Thugs would nab a rich man and contact the family with a ransom demand. The rich folks wanted to keep the cops and newspapers out of it, so they would quickly pay up and most times they would get their loved one back.

As kidnapping was not yet a federal crime, thugs knew it was a quick and usually clean way to make a lot of money. Many a rich man was snatched in the 1930s, and the public was not generally aware of it. Most families thought that silence was the way to go.

Lindbergh didn't keep silent. The report of the kidnapping created a frenzy. All cars entering or leaving New York City were stopped in the search for the baby. Colonel H. Norman Schwarzkopf—the father of the Gulf War general of the same name—headed up the command for the New Jersey State Police. With a naïve reverence, Schwarzkopf allowed Charles Lindbergh to lead the investigation, which was a foolish choice given the stress and worry the man was under.

A few days after the kidnapping, a seventy-two-year-old retired Bronx school principal, John F. Condon, wrote a letter to the *Bronx Home News* offering to act as an intermediary between Lindbergh and the kidnappers. He even offered to throw in an extra $1,000 of his own money if the baby was given to him. Condon was known as a blustery neighborhood character, and no one took him seriously. No one but Lindbergh and the kidnappers. Through newspaper ads, Condon—who used the moniker Jafsie for his initials, J.F.C.—was approved as the go-between.

On March 12, 1932 Condon and Lindbergh—with no police following as per Lindbergh's order—drove to 233rd Street and Jerome Avenue in the Bronx. They parked by the gates of Woodlawn Cemetery, and Condon got out and met a man wearing a fedora and a handkerchief over his face. Details of how to exchange the money were discussed, and Condon demanded he receive a token of the child's identity. A few days later a baby's suit was sent to Condon, and Lindbergh said it was his child's. Condon was sent another letter to set up a meeting, and he was advised to follow all of its instructions, as the kidnapping had been planned for over a year.

On the night of April 2, 1932 Condon and Lindbergh headed back to the Bronx to meet with the same man, who became known as "Graveyard John." They had $50,000 in gold certificates. They were allowed to meet the kidnapper with no police support because Lindbergh was almost mad with obsession with this case. But the FBI was not going to let him run the whole investigation. Behind Lindbergh's back an FBI agent had secretly recorded the serial numbers of the notes. Marking the bills made it easy to trace them when they were spent. Gold certificates were rare, and a list of the bills was given to all banks, large retail stores, and check-cashing operations.

Condon walked to the agreed meeting place and handed Graveyard John the case with the bills in it. Graveyard John told Condon the baby could be found on a boat docked on City Island in the East Bronx, then walked off into the woods by the cemetery and disappeared into the night.

Lindbergh sent out a posse of private investigators he had hired to scour City Island in search of his child. They found no boat or baby. It was all a lie. Lindbergh went home crushed. It would get worse. On May 12, 1932 the Lindbergh baby was found dead in the woods near his Hopewell, New Jersey house. The police brought Charles Lindbergh to the scene, and he stood over the body and declared it his son.

The man who handed over the cash to Graveyard John—John "Jafsie" Condon—became an immediate suspect and was vilified in the press. Cops suspected he may have been part of the scam and buried his share of the $50,000 in the backyard of his Bronx home. Condon invited the cops to search his home. They did, and found nothing. Condon wrote letters to the editor stating that he would not duck a fight. Condon claimed he was still in touch with the kidnappers and he would solve the crime himself.

From April of 1932 to September of 1934 the FBI had recovered $5,000 of the ransom money. It had been spent in stores, gas stations, and movie theaters in and around the New York area. The FBI tried to create a pattern of spending. All signs pointed to the Bronx, and "Jafsie" Condon again became a top suspect. Condon said he was too busy trying to solve the case to deal with the media and FBI speculation.

In September of 1934 the police got an anonymous phone tip that a Bronx man, Bruno Hauptmann of East 222nd Street, had some of the Lindbergh gold certificates. His house was searched and $13,760 of the Lindbergh money was found hidden in a trunk in his garage. Hauptmann acted surprised and said that the trunk belonged to a friend of his—a man named Fish—and that Fish had returned to Germany and had asked Hauptmann to hold the trunk for him. Hauptmann claimed he kept the trunk in the garage and never once looked inside. The police could not verify any man named Fish moving back to Germany, and as Hauptmann had no further information he was arrested for the Lindbergh kidnapping. An investigation on him went into full force.

Hauptmann was a thirty-five-year-old man from Saxony, Germany, who had a prison record in Germany. In July of 1923 he stowed away aboard the SS *Hanover* at Bremen, Germany. But the stowaway gambit didn't work: Hauptmann was arrested in the port of New York and deported. He tried again to get into America by boat in August, and again he was caught and deported.

But the third time was the charm, and Hauptmann successfully entered the United States on the *George Washington* in November of 1923. Two years later Hauptmann married an American waitress, Anna Schoeffler, and they had one son, Manford. Hauptmann was a carpenter by trade and worked in that field until March of 1932—right after the kidnapping. That month he quit the wood trade and began to speculate and trade stocks and bonds.

Hauptmann's former carpentry work was damning, because the ladder used to get into the Lindbergh nursery was believed to have been handmade by an experienced woodworker. The money in the trunk in the garage also looked bad, but Hauptmann claimed innocence. The problem was that Bruno Hauptmann appeared to be guilty of something.

His murder trial began on January 3, 1935 and lasted five weeks. The trial was a media circus and a big draw for spectators. People paid $500 to get a seat in the New Jersey courthouse. An elderly drunk who was two years away from an insane asylum defended Hauptmann.

Seeing that he was doomed, Hauptmann took the stand in his own defense and told the story that a friend of his named Fish had asked him to hold the money while Fish went back to Germany. He said he knew Fish died in Germany—something he had never told the cops—so Hauptmann reasoned that the money was his to spend. He told the jury he had spent very little of the loot in the trunk. He claimed he had no idea where the money came from, just that it was his friend's fortune.

So $5,000 was found spent in New York, and another $14,000 was recovered from Hauptmann's trunk. That left $31,000 in gold certificates that no one has ever found. The prosecutors and Hauptmann could never explain just where the rest of the money was or who else was involved with the kidnapping. Both sides were suspect, but only one would pay the price. While the jury was deliberating, crowds outside the courthouse chanted, "Kill Hauptmann . . . kill Hauptmann."

That they did. Hauptmann was found guilty and in Trenton, New Jersey on April 3, 1936 at 8:47 p.m. Bruno Hauptmann was electrocuted.

Now this leaves the question of what ever happened to the missing $31,000. The case is considered cold, and officially the FBI states that the gold certificates are still missing, but off the record FBI sources have admitted that after seventy-five years the gold certificates could have surfaced and been missed.

Through the years treasure seekers sought out "Jafsie" Condon's old house in the Bronx on Decatur Avenue. The man who bought it from Condon was seen by neighbors digging incessantly in the backyard. The man who now owns the old wood-frame house has also reported that every few years he had to call the cops because he spied odd-looking men lurking in his backyard and garage. He assumed they were looking for the Lindbergh money, because to this day tour buses still stop by and the tale of the missing money and Condon's role in the case is told in front of his door. A few years back Lindbergh buffs offered him money to dig around the house, but he has sent them all away. He figures if the missing money is still buried on the property it is hidden so well no one will ever find it.

So the Lindbergh case is marked officially solved, but the missing money is still out there. No one in law enforcement is pursuing the case, as the man who was arrested was executed for the crime. But even in 2007, $31,000 is a lot of money, so anyone with a spade and a strong back . . .

•••

One cold case, which is still open as the NYPD's oldest missing persons case, was blown open in 2005 by the *New York Post*.

This old chestnut started in the summer of 1930 when a New York Supreme Court judge, Joseph F. Crater, was at his vacation home in Belgrade Lakes, Maine. He got a phone call that disturbed him. Crater was a mover and a shaker in the fast-paced world of New York politics. Word was out that Crater had bought his judge seat, and the man to whom he had given the bribe money was about to go to the cops with the information. Crater told his wife, Stella, that he would have to return to New York City to "straighten some fellow out."

Crater was born in Easton, Pennsylvania, and had come to New York for law school. He loved the fast life of the city and fit right in. Crater didn't enter politics for the public good. After he became leader of the Democratic Party in New York, his law firm made a fortune off of work from the party and from city contracts. Then New York governor Franklin Delano Roosevelt appointed him as a state Supreme Court judge. Roosevelt didn't really care who was a judge and he appointed whomever the Democratic Party told him to. FDR knew nothing of Crater's skullduggery, and the appointment was pro forma. Crater knew how to play the game, and he had taken out $20,000 from his savings account the week before he was named judge. It was rumored that $20,000 was the going rate to the local Dem leaders to buy a judgeship in New York.

Crater had been a judge in New York's Supreme Court for only four months when he heard that his bribery scheme was about to be exposed. Crater came back to New York, and on August 6, 1930 he left a Broadway chophouse and waved goodbye to some friends. He got into a waiting cab, and that was the last time he was ever seen.

Among several underground crime sources it was said that Crater was killed in case he decided to have loose lips. An investigation was coming, and many felt that Crater was a novice in the cop and corruption game and would not be able to keep his mouth shut.

When he didn't return to Maine after two weeks, his wife grew worried. She called their friends in New York, but no one had seen him. When the Manhattan Supreme Court opened—it had closed for most of the summer—on August 25, and Crater did not appear, judge friends grew concerned and started their own internal investigation. No one wanted to involve the cops because Crater and his pals were into a lot of shady dealings.

After a week doing their own investigations, the judges finally called in the NYPD, and the cops began to look into Judge Joseph F. Crater. His private bank boxes were empty, and the files in his office were gone. "Ransacked" was how one cop described it, as if Crater—or his killers—were in a hurry to get rid of evidence.

Crater seemed to have been hiding something. It turned out that he was, and in 1931 the Seabury Commission was set up to investigate the widespread corruption of New York politics. Its first job was to chase New York Mayor Jimmy Walker out of New York, along with scores of other corrupt democrats. Evidence came out about how judgeships were bought and sold, and had Crater been around, he probably would have—at minimum—lost his judgeship.

But he never did come back. He became a tabloid punch line and was called "the most missingest man in America." In 1939 his wife had him declared legally dead so she could collect on his life insurance policies. For years afterward, on every August 6 she would go to a bar in Greenwich Village and order two drinks. She would drink one and leave the other on the bar and look at it as she toasted to the air, saying, "For wherever you are, Joe."

This was where the tale stopped, until seventy-five years later when in August of 2005 the *New York Post* told the story that the NYPD's cold case squad was looking into the Judge Crater case—its oldest missing persons case.

The break came in April of 2005 when a ninety-one-year-old great-grandmother, Stella Ferrucci-Good, died in Bellerose, Queens. Her forty-six-year-old granddaughter, Barbara O'Brien, found a letter while going through her grandma's things. There was writing on the envelope in red pen: "Do Not Open Until I Am Dead."

O'Brien read the letter and couldn't believe it. Her grandmother wrote that her dead husband, Robert Good, and an NYPD cop named Charles Burns had killed Judge Crater and buried him under the boardwalk by West 8th Street in Coney Island, Brooklyn. Ferrucci-Good expressed guilt over holding onto this knowledge for all these years. Along with the letter were yellowed newspaper clippings about Crater.

The NYPD took this very seriously. They knew that the remains of five humans had been found near that part of the boardwalk back in the 1950s when an aquarium was build there. The NYPD sent out forensic experts to see if the exhumed remains could be traced to the missing judge. The remains had been buried on Harts Island in Potter's Field, and it was doubtful if the exact burial spot could be identified.

This is where the case hit a snag. No records were found to describe in just what part of the Potter's Field the remains had been buried. The NYPD researched the case hard because they knew the media was looking over their shoulders. But the island was too vast, and the remains could not be found. The NYPD holds out hope that if any future work is done by the old Brooklyn boardwalk, they will be called first to look for remains.

So Judge Crater—even in death—eludes ever being found. The best lead on the case creates another mystery, and if the story is to be believed, Crater lies among other scores of unknown people.

•••

Judge Crater's is a cold, cold case, but in Atlanta in 2005 a case involving a judge was hot—very hot.

When Brian Nichols, thirty-three, appeared at the Fulton County Courthouse in Atlanta on March 12, 2005, it was not for the trial of the century. There was no missing money, and no media covered his trial. Nichols was just another of America's thousands of anonymous felons. This was all about to change.

Nichols had the capacity for extreme violence. Just two days earlier, a sheriff's deputy had found two makeshift weapons on Nichols. The presiding judge, Rowland Barnes, had a meeting with the attorneys and promised that there would be more security for Nichols's trial. The attorneys claim they never saw an increase of security inside the courtroom.

Nichols was in court on rape charges. He had kidnapped his ex-girlfriend and tied her up with duct tape. He raped her for three straight days until her birthday. It was some kind of sick and twisted birthday present. Nichols had brought a cooler of food with him to keep up his strength during the attack. His ex—a Fortune 500 executive—filed a complaint against him and police arrested him. Nichols's defense was that the sex had been consensual.

His first trial on those charges had wound up in a hung jury, and Nichols was afraid that this jury was not going to be so undecided. The charges were heavy enough that he was facing life in prison and was a desperate man.

Deputy Cynthia Hall, fifty-one, guarded Nichols in a room near the court. Hall was a grandmother and very small. She was all alone in a room with a burly felon who was a college football linebacker. This was the first bit of insanity in this case.

Brian Nichols was not handcuffed as he put on his suit for his court appearance. He saw an opportunity and proceeded to attack

Deputy Hall. She fought a good fight, but Nichols overpowered her. He knocked her out—she would be hospitalized later in critical condition, but she did survive—and locked her in the holding room. He took her keys and a 9 mm gun and headed for the courtroom, which was on the other side of a long hallway.

At about 9:20 a.m. Nichols coolly walked into Barnes's courtroom and shot Judge Barnes dead before anyone knew something was wrong. Nichols then shot court reporter Julie Ann Brandau dead and herded the cowering lawyers and other court workers into a back room and locked them in.

Nichols took off on foot. At the courthouse exit Deputy Hoyt Teasley, forty-three, tried to stop him. It was the last police action Teasley would take. Nichols shot him dead and fled into an Atlanta subway station and took a train heading north.

Atlanta went wild after this attack. A cold blooded killer was loose, and no one was safe. A call came over the police radios that Nichols had carjacked a green Honda Accord that belonged to an Atlanta reporter. Cops wasted their time looking for the green car. Nichols had escaped on foot and then a train and was now miles away from where the cops were searching.

About 10 miles outside of Atlanta Nichols found David Wilhelm outside his home doing some yard work. He shot Wilhelm dead, and hit pay dirt: Wilhelm was a federal agent, and now Nichols had a second gun, a federal badge, and a pickup truck.

Nichols drove to Gwinnett County and pulled the truck into an apartment building parking lot. There he spied Ashley Smith, twenty-six, walking to her apartment. He grabbed her and forced himself into her home. There he tied her up and took a shower.

Nichols was now exhausted and talked with Smith. He told her he wanted to give up and do no more killing. Smith told him of her struggle as a methamphetamine addict. Smith begged Nichols to let her go so she could see her daughter. She told him that the girl's dad was dead, and if he killed Smith, she would be an orphan.

Nichols felt connected with Smith. They talked about God and hope, and then she made him pancakes. As the night wore on, Nichols had mercy and let the plucky hostage go. Of course, she immediately called the police, and Nichols watched on TV as a SWAT team surrounded the apartment. He had no more fight in him. Now he was outmanned and outgunned. He waved a white shirt out the window in surrender and was taken into custody.

The mystery of Brian Nichols was that he was not your ordinary street thug. He was brought up in a stable, middle-class family. He attended college at Kutztown University in Pennsylvania. He played linebacker for the football team. But Nichols had some problems with school and left the college after two years.

His family claimed that he had a very good job as a computer engineer and was making a six-figure income. His record showed that before the rape arrest, he had only one other arrest for a misdemeanor burglary ten years before. The Nichols family assumed that mental illness led to the crime spree.

Nichols has pled not guilty to all of the charges stemming from the courthouse incident. He goes to trial in the summer of 2007.

Atlanta learned from this major security snafu. Now the hallways and courtrooms have added armed deputies. Prisoners must be escorted by at least two officers. One officer is unarmed with the prisoner, and the other officer stands out of the enclosed area and remains armed. He never leaves his partner alone, and that move in itself would have stopped Brian Nichols's killing spree. It is a bit like locking the barn after the horse is stolen, but with these small steps Atlanta courts have remained safe.

•••

At the opposite end from Brian Nichols and the Atlanta court system was another hot case of two desperate Bloods gang members on trial in a Brooklyn courthouse. They would have done what Nichols did if they could have gotten away with it.

In January of 2006 Troy Hendrix, twenty-two, and Kayson Pearson, twenty-four, were on trial for their miserable lives in the Brooklyn Supreme Court. They were members of the Bloods street gang, and their crimes were heinous. They had kidnapped a college student, Ramona Moore, twenty-one, and taken her to an abandoned apartment building in Bedford-Stuyvesant. They tied her up, raped her, strangled her to death, and then burned her body to hide their deed.

Ramona Moore was everything these two fiends were not. She was a woman from the ghetto who was trying to improve herself. She wanted more from life, but these two losers made sure she never saw that.

While on trial, Hendrix and Pearson came up with a plan. They smuggled in two sharpened plastic knives, and during a break in the trial Pearson jumped up and attacked his attorney, Mitchell Dinnerstein. The two fought and fell to the ground. Pearson struck Dinnerstein three times on his head, causing minor injuries. While Pearson was beating on his lawyer, Troy Hendrix saw his chance and rushed the bench. Judge Albert Tomei yelled out, "Holy shit!"

Troy Hendrix jumped on a court officer, Sergeant James Gorra, standing in front of the judge and grabbed for his 9 mm weapon. Cops and court officers are trained to retain their weapons no matter what. You don't need an active imagination to foresee what Troy Hendrix would do with a gun in a crowded courtroom. Gorra was able to beat Hendrix back, and other officers grabbed him and got the two prisoners under control. The two felons were led back to their cells, and court was adjourned for the day.

Hendrix and Pearson later claimed they were not trying to escape but rather they wanted the court officers to kill them so they wouldn't have to face a life sentence. It didn't work. Later in the year they received life without parole plus twenty-two years for their escape attempt.

sporting criminals

THE NAMES OF SPORTS FIGURES often turn up in reports on the police blotter. Maybe it's because the pressures of big money and big fame lead to misbehavior. Young athletes end up running with entourages that include sketchy characters. Aggression that should have been left on the field gets fueled with booze, and the next thing you know some star athlete has smashed, crashed, or bashed his way onto the police blotter.

Terry "Tank" Johnson of the Chicago Bears has been a big hit on the police blotter. In February of 2006, Johnson was in Chicago getting his freak on at a nightclub called The Level. He left the club at 3:45 a.m. and saw a Chicago police officer ticketing his limo for blocking traffic.

Johnson took great offense at this and lumbered up to the cop. According to the police report, Johnson yelled at the cop, "You ain't the only one with a Glock. If it wasn't for your gun and badge I'd kick your ass."

The officer proceeded to call for backup, and when Johnson resisted arrest, the police officer had to spray mace at the big Bear. Four cops wrestled him to the ground and handcuffed him. He had no weapons on him or in his car, but he was charged with resisting arrest and disorderly conduct.

The charges were later dropped, but Johnson couldn't keep out of trouble. In December of 2006 police received an anonymous tip on a cache of weapons housed in Tank Johnson's home in Gurnee, Illinois. Cops raided Chez Johnson and found three rifles, three handguns, and scores of boxes of ammunition. The guns and ammo were confiscated, and Johnson was charged with ten counts of illegal weapons possession. He made bail, but he had to get a court order to travel with the Bears to Miami so he could play in the Super Bowl. He and his team did not do well in that game.

In March of 2007 Johnson was sent to an Illinois jail for two months on the weapons charges. The NFL suspended Johnson for the first eight games of the 2007 season. The Chicago Bears made it clear to Johnson that this would be his last chance.

Johnson was released from prison in May of 2007 and swore in an interview that he would fly right from now on. He knew he had one last chance, and he didn't want to blow it. He went to his second house in Arizona hoping to live quietly. That lasted about a month. In June he was speeding around in Gilbert, Arizona, a suburb outside of Phoenix. According to the police report, Johnson was doing 64 miles per hour in a 40 mph zone. When the cop asked him to step outside of the car, he looked drunk. He was arrested, and Sergeant Andrew Duncan said that Johnson was arrested for "DUI, impaired to the slightest degree."

Johnson was released by the cops, and the Chicago Bears were inspired. They also released Johnson. Chicago general manager Jerry Angelo said, "We are upset and embarrassed by Tank's actions. He compromised the credibility of our organization. We made it clear to him that he had no room for error."

As of July 2007, Johnson is out of football. He can't play for the first half of 2007 should a team pick him up. It could be worse—at least Johnson is still alive.

•••

One of the most shocking NFL police blotter tales in 2007 was the drive-by killing of Darrent Williams of the Denver Broncos. Twelve hours after his team played their last game of the season, Williams, twenty-four, was shot dead.

The game that night was a bitter loss to the San Francisco 49ers. Williams had a good season, but was let down by the play of his team. He left Mile High Stadium to go to a Denver nightclub called The Shelter to celebrate New Year's Eve with two NBA stars—Kenyon Martin and Carmelo Anthony of the Denver Nuggets. At the party witnesses recall that some people got into a scuffle with gang members trying to crash the club. The witnesses stated that Williams was not involved in the fight. Denver police later looked at all of the club's security videos, but saw no fight.

By all accounts Darrent Williams was a good man. He was raising his two children back in his hometown of Fort Worth, Texas, and had plans to start a foundation to keep young kids out of gangs. According to the Denver PD, at 2:00 a.m. Williams was in the backseat of a leased Hummer with his teammate Javon Walker. Driving the vehicle was Brandon Flowers, and in the front passenger seat sat Nicole Reindel—all friends of Williams.

Williams took out his Blackberry and was about to text message his mother in Fort Worth when a single bullet struck him in the neck. He fell into Javon Walker's lap. The Denver medical examiner said that Williams died instantly from the bullet, and he was completely sober when he died. The shooters drove a beat-up 1998 SUV and lit up the Hummer with twelve gunshots. Only Walker was not hit.

Brandon Flowers, Nicole Reindel, and Williams were rushed to a local hospital where Williams was pronounced dead. Flowers and Reindel recovered from their wounds. None of the people with Williams knew why the car had been targeted. There had been no argument.

There was no incident on the road. It was like the SUV pulled out into the night and started shooting for no apparent reason.

The Denver PD had a different theory. Gang activity has increased in Denver over the last few years. A major case was being worked on a gang called the Tre Tre gang—an offshoot of the Crips in Los Angeles. The Denver PD thought that some gang members may have shot at Williams in a case of mistaken identity. This theory may hold up, because five days after Williams was killed, the Denver PD made a major bust of more than fifty members of the Tre Tre for drug dealing and weapons possession charges. They had a number of men in custody from the gang who the police labeled as "persons of interest."

One Tre Tre gang member, Brian Hicks, twenty-nine, was already in jail for attempted murder. Hicks was in prison when Williams was shot, but the Denver PD found the abandoned SUV that was used in the drive-by killing. It was registered to Hicks.

All of the arrested gang members claimed they had no knowledge of the Darrent Williams shooting. As of July of 2007, the Denver PD still hasn't charged anyone in the murder. The Denver Broncos have put up a $100,000 reward for information leading to the arrest and conviction of Williams's killer, but so far no one has stepped up to claim the money. Darrent Williams's murder remains unsolved.

•••

In April of 2007 some hockey players got into the police blotter mix. On April 7, 2007 two Florida Panthers hockey players went to a Miami nightclub to drown their sorrows over a disappointing season. Goalie Ed Belfour and forward Ville Peltonen were at the Nikki Beach Bar when some patrons complained to the bouncers about the loutish behavior of the two hockey goons.

The bouncers approached Belfour and Peltonen and asked them to leave. The players refused, and the bouncers called the Miami PD. The players then left, but were met outside the club by a

Miami cop who asked to see some identification. The cop's report stated that Belfour "walked forward in a fighting stance."

The Miami PD was not going to mess around with these guys. The cop tasered Belfour, who fell to the ground screaming. Peltonen had run to a nearby Miami firetruck and broke a metal shaft off the vehicle to fight the cops. When he saw Belfour being tasered, he thought better of it and dropped the pole.

The two men were arrested and then released on $1,500 bail. It came out that Belfour was no stranger to the police blotter. On Halloween of 2000 in Dallas, Texas, Belfour was arrested for attacking a security guard in a hotel. When the Dallas PD handcuffed him, he drunkenly offered the cops $100,000 to let him go. When the cops laughed at his offer, he upped it to a billion dollars. Belfour was lucky he wasn't charged with bribery, and was only charged with misdemeanor and paid a fine.

In May of 2007 the two NHL players accepted a deal in a Miami-Dade County courtroom. They were sentenced to twenty hours of community service and had to pay $200 to the Miami Police Athletic League—which is a police-sponsored program that gets kids involved in sports instead of crime. The two players also had to apologize to the cops. The Florida Panthers issued no statement, but word is that goalie Ed Belfour has played his last game for the Florida Panthers. In the 2007 NHL draft the Panthers took a hot, young, and hopefully sober goalie.

•••

Former baseball player Jeff Reardon had a stellar career as a major league relief pitcher and was ranked sixth on the all-time list for saves by a reliever when he retired in 1994. He had never been in trouble with the cops and was leading a quiet life of retirement in Florida. In 2005, that must have become quiet desperation because Reardon hit the police blotter in an unbelievable fashion.

On December 26, 2005 Reardon walked into Hamilton Jewelers at a mall in Palm Beach, Florida. He handed the store manager a note that read, "I have a gun please place $100 bills and jewelry in a bag and no one will get hurt. Thank you."

The manager put $170 in a bag and Reardon grabbed the loot and walked out. He ambled a few stores down and went inside a restaurant and sat down. That was where the Palm Beach PD found him. The cops came in and ordered Reardon to stand up. He did, and began walking toward the cop. The officer pointed a gun at Reardon and told him to stop. The cop later said it was like Reardon woke up and immediately began to comply with his orders.

Lieutenant David O'Neil said Reardon offered no resistance. He was charged by police with armed robbery even though he had no gun on him. O'Neil told an Orlando reporter that Reardon said, "It was the medication that made him do it and that he was sorry." The police report quoted Reardon as saying, "I'm sorry. I did it. I robbed them. I didn't know what I was doing. I'm out of my mind. It's the medication. I'm sorry."

Reardon was booked, arraigned, and released on $5,000 bail. Now the question of why Reardon robbed the store begged to be answered. He had $500 in his wallet when he went into the jewelry store. Reardon had earned about $11 million dollars while playing baseball and had invested his money wisely. He had no pressing financial problems. It turned out that Reardon's problem was with his heart.

Reardon and his wife, Phebe, had three kids. Their middle child, Shane, was a troubled young man. He had severe drug problems, and the Reardons finally enrolled him in a drug treatment program where he seemed to thrive. But it wouldn't last. In February of 2004 Shane Reardon, twenty, was dead from a drug overdose.

Phebe Reardon suffered, but somehow held up. Her husband wasn't as strong. Jeff Reardon fell into a dark depression. He told his wife that he wished it was he that was dead instead of Shane. He claimed he had a broken heart. Reardon left behind golf and fishing—two things he loved. He would spend his days lying on Shane's bed mulling over where he had gone wrong. He only got up to go on the Internet and blog on a Web site set up for Shane Reardon. On the message board were countless missives from Jeff Reardon to his son.

"Please come home, we need you with us."

"Things are still really rough without you."

Jeff Reardon's last posting before his jewelry store robbery was written on November 26, 2005.

"Dear Shaner,

I miss you more than ever. Can't stop thinking about you.

Love You,

DAD"

On December 22, 2005 Jeff Reardon was admitted to a Florida hospital. He constantly told doctors his heart was broken from Shane's death. His heart also had a severe blockage, and he was admitted for an angioplasty—his third such procedure. He was released from the hospital a day later and was on ten different medications for his heart ailment and his depression.

Reardon's lawyer, Mitch Beer, claimed that all those meds caused his client to act in such a bizarre way. After his arrest Reardon's family checked him into a mental hospital where he would receive twenty-four-hour care for his depression.

The hospital care seemed to work. In August of 2006 Jeff Reardon was found not guilty by reason of insanity by circuit court judge Stephen Rapp. Rapp ordered Reardon to appear before him every six months, and so far Reardon seems to have regained some of his life.

•••

Brooklyn Dodger Len Koenecke was a true police blotter original. Along with his baseball exploits, he was the man credited with the first attempted hijacking of an American airplane.

In 1930 Koenecke was a promising baseball prospect who worked as a railroad fireman in Wisconsin during the off-season. He claimed the railroad job kept him in good shape. In 1930 Koenecke signed on with the Buffalo Bisons—a respected minor league team—and had some good years there. The Bisons must have appreciated him, because today you can hit eBay's auction site and bid on an old Len Koenecke jigsaw puzzle that was given away in 1930 as a gimmick by the Bisons to get fans to come out to the ballpark.

A puzzle is a fitting tribute to a man no one was ever able to figure out. To his wife, his managers, and his teammates, he remained an enigma. When news of his big day came out in the police blotter everyone was stunned. He was a wild and wooly guy sometimes, but hijacking a plane? No one saw that coming. His baseball managers may have best understood him when they described Koenecke—when they were feeling generous—as a mercurial character.

In 1931 fortune smiled upon Len Koenecke. The New York Giants liked what they saw in him and paid $75,000 to Buffalo for his contract. But Koenecke was a big league bust who earned a bad name in the clubhouse for being a hothead and a flake.

He was sent back to the minors and lingered there for a few years. He got another shot at the majors in 1934 when the Brooklyn Dodgers bought his contract for $35,000. This time Koenecke would not disappoint, and he batted a solid .320 for the year and was the league's best center fielder with a fielding percentage of .994.

Koenecke's only strong major league year was 1934. In 1935 he struggled all season and annoyed his teammates and manager with his locker room eccentricities. He constantly complained that his spikes hurt his feet. His rituals before the game and his incessant chatter drove them nuts. He had to have everything his way.

Toward the end of the season on September 15, 1935, at an away game against the Chicago Cubs, Brooklyn Dodgers manager Casey Stengel had grown weary of Koenecke's weak batting and boneheaded fielding plays. Stengel gave him one last shot that day as a pinch hitter. It was do or die for Koenecke. He came up in the ninth inning with the game on the line, and all Koenecke could manage was a weak groundout. The next day in the team hotel Stengel called him to his room. Without a smile he ordered Koenecke to pack his bags and go home. He was cut from the team, and it looked like his baseball career was over.

Koenecke stormed out of the hotel in Chicago and caught an American Airlines flight to Detroit. As the plane took off, he broke out a quart of whiskey and proceeded to drink his baseball blues away. In short order Koenecke was stinking drunk, grabbing at the flight attendant and insulting fellow passengers. He got so wound up that the pilot came back to the cabin and ordered Koenecke to be shackled to his seat. The pilot sat on him while the copilot wrapped chains around him.

In Detroit, Koenecke left the airplane unconscious. He was laid down in a terminal and allowed to sleep off the alcohol. When he woke up, he bought a ticket on a charter flight for Toronto. On that flight, things got bad.

He continued drinking while aboard, and as the small plane flew 2,000 feet over Canada, Koenecke crashed into the cockpit and assaulted the pilot and copilot. Shoving the pilot aside, he grabbed the stick and tried to commandeer the plane. The pilot picked up a nearby fire extinguisher and bashed in Koenecke's skull.

The pilot and copilot made a crash landing on a racetrack. Koenecke was no longer breathing. The police arrived, and after pronouncing Koenecke dead, they arrested the pilot and copilot for manslaughter. After holding the two flyers in jail for five days, the police had enough proof that the two pilots had acted in self-defense and released them.

At twenty-seven, Len Koenecke was dead. He would be remembered only as the nutty Dodger who tried to hijack an airplane and got his head bashed in for his trouble.

•••

Warren Wells sprang out of the Southeastern Texas town of Beaumont, to become a fleet-footed wide receiver who lit the AFL on fire in the late 1960s. Wells was one of sixteen pro football players who came out of Beaumont during that time. Along with Wells were Bubba Smith, Jess Phillips, and Mel and Miller Farr. Between them they had eleven Pro Bowl appearances. In 1971 that city decided to name itself "the Pro Football Capital of the World," and that same year CBS did a special report on Beaumont, calling the town "the Pipeline to the AFL."

Beaumont is a hardscrabble town of 120,000, and it truly is amazing that it has produced as many pro football players as it has. But they take the game seriously down there. While Warren Wells may have been one of the best receivers to come out of that football garden, he was certainly one of the sorriest criminals to ever disgrace Beaumont.

If you watch ESPN's Classic Sports channel, you can still see old Oakland Raiders clips of Wells catching a long spiral pass from Daryl "The Mad Bomber" Lamonica. Those two were the Peyton Manning and Marvin Harrison of their day. Wells always had a knack for finding the end zone, and in three years he scored thirty-one touchdowns for the high-scoring Raiders.

In 1969 after two consecutive thousand-yard seasons, Warren Wells hit the police blotter hard. He was arrested for rape. The charges were later lowered to aggravated assault, and Wells was given probation. It didn't help. The damage was done, and the NFL was nervous.

The cops seemed to have it in for Wells. In 1970 while he was drinking in a bar, a woman stabbed him in the chest. He was trying to pick her up and she felt he was being rude, so she pulled out her knife and gave him a stick. She ran out of the bar and fled. Friends took Wells to the hospital, and when he tried to report the knife attack to the police, they arrested him for violating his probation. He was drinking, and sobriety was one of the conditions of his freedom. In 1971 he did ten months in a California jail for the violation, and when he was released from prison, he walked away from football.

There weren't a whole lot of job opportunities for fleet-footed receivers away from the gridiron, so Wells returned to Beaumont. In 1976 he was arrested for burglary while out panhandling on Beaumont's main drag. Wells was considered a lost cause by his former teammates, and with this charge and others Wells was in and out of the Texas prisons on skid bids—short sentences for petty crimes. Sportswriters who had covered his gridiron exploits couldn't be bothered with his criminal career.

Today Warren Wells still lives in Beaumont with relatives and haunts the town with the broken promise of his youth. He now looks well worn, and it is hard to imagine this broken-down man pulling in a touchdown pass. He spends most of his days drinking and cadging money from the locals.

One of his old friends, Enous Minix, once told a Dallas reporter, "I see Warren practically every day. As a high school student he was one of the nicest people you could imagine. I don't know what happened. He is still struggling."

•••

Reggie Harding has to be one of the few seven-foot-tall men to take to crime. Most seven-footers realize that being such a tall drink of water makes you susceptible to being picked out of police lineups.

In 1963 Harding made his NBA debut with the Detroit Pistons. He had a great career in front of him. He was the first player to be drafted out of high school to go into the NBA. He was a high school phenom in Detroit and looked forward to pitting his muscular 260 pounds against the best big men the NBA had to offer.

The Motor City had high hopes for the strapping lad, and many were thinking that Harding just might be the new Wilt Chamberlain. He wasn't. He put up some decent numbers, but his frequent bouts with a drinking problem and his penchant for petty crime got him thrown off the Pistons. Back in those days, the standards for players' conduct were probably just as tough as they are today, but trouble-makers stood out more in a basketball world that—mostly—behaved itself in public and on the court.

Harding worked his way over to Chicago until the Bulls also cut him. He went back home to Detroit, and the police arrested him on a burglary charge. When told of the arrest, an NBA general manager described Reggie Harding as "seven feet of trouble."

After his jail bid, Harding got one more shot at a basketball career. In 1967 the newly formed Indiana Pacers of the American Basketball Association knew all about Harding's bad rep and criminal ways, but they were desperate for a center with thirty games left to play in the season. The Pacers GM, Mike Storem, met Harding at an airport the day he was released from prison and offered him a contract. Harding signed it, and in a short while they both regretted the move.

On one of Harding's first road trips for the Pacers he was paired with a nervous white forward named Jim Rayl. The night before a big game Rayl was asleep when he sensed that Harding was sitting on his bed. He turned on the light, and he saw Harding pointing a gun at his head. Harding gave Rayl a smile and said, "I heard you don't like niggers."

Somehow Rayl was able to talk some sense into Harding. Harding calmed down and handed the gun to Rayl and went back to his bed. Rayl unloaded the gun and put the bullets under his pillow. He gave the gun back to Harding, said goodnight, and shut off the light. A few minutes later Rayl heard Harding moving around the room. Rayl turned on the light and saw Harding reloading the gun. Harding smiled and asked Rayl, "You didn't think I only had six bullets?"

Rayl did not get much sleep, but luckily survived the night. In the morning he ran to the coach and demanded to have a new roommate. Harding was allowed to room alone after that.

On the team's off-days Reggie Harding refused to practice with the other Pacers. During games he would put himself in and take himself out of games whenever he felt like it. He didn't care what the coach had to say about it. He was playing well and was averaging thirteen points a game and thirteen rebounds, but the Indiana Pacers grew weary of him and at the end of the season they sent him packing.

Harding responded by appearing on a local TV show, threatening to shoot Pacers' general manager Mike Storem dead. After that threat Harding would never play another game of professional basketball.

After the 1967 season he returned home to Detroit, and when things got tight, he would rob liquor stores. He hit the police blotter when he went into a liquor store where he was a regular Muscatel—cheap wine—buyer. Harding put a ski mask over his face and pointed a gun in the owner's face.

"Give me all your money! Now!" Harding yelled.

"Reggie, I know it's you," the owner said with a weary voice, throwing down the newspaper he was reading.

Harding ran out the door, saying, "No, man, it ain't me."

The owner didn't even bother to call the police. Everyone had a good laugh at the big goofball's foolishness. But Harding's life was fast devolving. He became a hard-core heroin addict, and all the laughs ended on September 2, 1972. On that day Harding was hanging out on a Detroit street known as a hot drug spot. A car with two men in the front stopped, and one of the men called Harding over. The big man bent down to talk, and someone shot him three times. He fell into the street, and the car pulled away. The unreliable witnesses—addicts and dealers—did not get the license plate number of the car.

Harding died in the streets of Detroit. The cops wondered how Harding lived as long as he did. He was always fighting and robbing the people he knew in his hometown. It was only a matter of time before someone got ticked off enough to decide that the ex-NBA star had squandered a career and wasn't going to make a living as a hood. No one was ever charged with the killing. The Detroit PD investigated the shooting but came up with loose ends. Just like Harding's life.

•••

Baseball player Hank Thompson pulled himself out of a troubled youth of crime and poverty in Oklahoma City to achieve a starring role in the legendary Negro League. He had grown up as a restless juvenile delinquent who often tried to go straight, and at times he could, but he never was far from trouble. It seemed to follow him.

Thompson played for the Kansas City Monarchs. Drafted into the army during World War II, he served as a machine gunner and proved himself a good soldier in the Battle of the Bulge. After the war he went back to the Negro League and then was drafted into the National League by the New York Giants. As long as he could hit a baseball, someone would always bail him out when he got in trouble.

Thompson was a solid-hitting and good-fielding slugger. He had the nickname "Hammerin' Hank" years before Hank Aaron earned that same moniker. But, perhaps most notably, he teamed up with Willie Mays and Monte Irvin in the outfield, forming the first all-black outfield on a major league baseball team. Like all good things, however, great baseball careers tend to end far too early.

Thompson had a .267 lifetime average with 129 career home runs. He hit .364 in the 1954 World Series when the Giants swept the Cleveland Indians. And Thompson was also the first black batter to face a black pitcher, Brooklyn Dodgers ace Don Newcombe.

But when baseball ended, Hank Thompson fell back on a career that had begun when he was young: he was first arrested at age eleven for breaking and entering. As a teen he added a few more arrests, and at twenty-two he was arrested for killing a man in a barroom fight. In 1953 when he played for the New York Giants, he was arrested for beating up a cab driver. Most of Thompson's problems stemmed from a lifelong addiction to alcohol.

His drinking took its toll on his body, and by thirty-two Thompson had become old overnight. He was cut from the Giants, and he was in no shape to play any more baseball. When Thompson left baseball, he became a lost man, haunting the old Harlem neighborhood that his team had fled in 1957 for the Western promise of San Francisco. His drinking got worse. He became morose, and his wife had to leave him because she couldn't take any more of his drunken rages. Her departure only made him worse, and he told friends he had nothing to live for.

With all this hurt behind him in 1961, on a lazy spring afternoon in Harlem—just blocks away from the Polo Grounds where he starred as a Giant—Thompson, age thirty-five, walked into an empty bar called Bill's Café. The bartender wiped the bar with a white towel and asked him what he was having.

Thompson looked out the door with a nervous glance and then with a small smile said, "Do you know who I am?"

The bartender smiled back and figured him for an old friend. He put down his towel and took a good look at the man. He told him that he was sorry but he didn't recognize him.

"Good!" Thompson said and pulled out a .22 caliber pistol from his waistband and blurted, "This is a stickup. Put the money on the bar."

With the barrel of the gun following him to the cash register, the bartender meekly punched open the machine and dumped the money out on the wooden bar. Thompson scooped up the dollars and stuffed them into his pocket. He backed out of the bar and then ran into the street. The bartender called the local precinct with a solid description of the stickup man, and the cops were able to catch Thompson ten blocks away.

The incident was just another New York City stickup and probably wouldn't have been mentioned in any of the newspapers. But not only did it make the crime blotters, the sports section grabbed it too. The headlines blared that a stickup man in Harlem had once been the Giants star known as Hammerin' Hank Thompson.

After his arrest for holding up Bill's Café, Thompson was sitting in the Tombs waiting to be charged with armed robbery when Horace Stoneman, the Giants owner, flew in from San Francisco and bailed Thompson out. Stoneman also got the judge to sentence him to two years' probation. Of course, Stoneman didn't offer Thompson a job—just a get-out-of-jail card. When asked why he robbed a bar, Thompson said that he was going to use the money for a bus ticket to Fresno, California, to visit his sick mom.

Thompson actually did cobble together the money to go see his sick mother. But by 1963 he was back in the blotter when Houston cops busted him for a $270 liquor store heist. This was his seventh arrest, so Texas saw fit to give him a ten-year sentence. Realizing that alcohol had fueled most of his crimes, Thompson joined AA in jail, and by all reports he became a model prisoner. He was paroled in 1968, and he moved back to Fresno to start a new life. He got a job as a playground director and was trying to get a front office job in baseball when he had a seizure and died in 1969. He was all of forty-three when he died.

•••

You might think you don't know who Rollen Stewart is, but you probably do know him. If you watched any sports on TV in the 1970s and '80s, he was the multicolored Afro-wig-wearing nut who held up the big sign with the Bible citation, "John 3:16."

If you ever wondered just what Stewart was selling with that logo, it was from the Book of John, chapter 3, verse 16: "For God so loved the world, that He gave His only begotten Son, that whosoever believeth in Him should not perish but have everlasting life."

Stewart definitely got everlasting life in the earthly sense: he wound up being sentenced to three concurrent life sentences in a California prison after a 1992 incident. You see, after Stewart gave up his sign and wig in the '80s, he wanted to become an evangelist. No one was getting his message, and Stewart turned ugly.

Stewart was suspected of igniting stink bombs at various sporting events. In 1992, he took over a Hyatt hotel room near the Los Angeles airport, taking a maid as hostage and locking himself and her in the room. He started small fires and called the police on himself.

Soon Stewart had all the attention he craved. He put signs out on the windows with scripture verses. He told the cops that he had a bomb, so LAPD sent its SWAT team in and they tried to negotiate with Stewart. The would-be evangelist told SWAT he would set off three bombs if he wasn't given airtime on all the TV stations in Los Angeles.

When the cops were slow to meet his demands, he threatened to shoot at incoming planes at LAX airport with a .45 mm handgun. That little promise convinced the LAPD to take action, and the cops broke through the door and took Stewart down with stun grenades. They cuffed him and hauled him off before he fired a single shot. They found the maid weeping in the bathroom, unharmed.

Stewart had a lengthy trial, and he acted unruly through most of it. The DA easily proved Stewart's guilt. The Jesus nut's threat to shoot airplanes did him in. He had the opportunity and positioning to do it in the room at the Hyatt, and he had a weapon that could penetrate a plane's metal body.

The jury agreed with the DA and did not take kindly to Stewart's antics in court. When the guilty verdict came down and Stewart got three consecutive life sentences, he threw himself to the ground and claimed the court was prejudiced against Jesus Christ.

In an interview for the book *Sports Fans Who Made Headlines*, Stewart was asked about his life in prison. He was doing his time at the California State Prison in Represa, California.

"I was in a position where I had an audience of 2.8 billion through satellite dishes. Now I can only spread my faith in the yard to criminals who consider me a woman."

He must still have been wearing the rainbow wig.

But Stewart wasn't done with us. In January of 2001 he sent out a public letter to a newspaper. He wrote it with crayons, and in religious gibberish he claimed the world would end on September 18, 2001. While he was off by only seven days for the apocalyptic scenes of lower Manhattan, the Pentagon, and central Pennsylvania, Stewart himself was still waiting for parole on September 18. He had a parole hearing in 2004 and was denied. At sixty-two he continues to serve his sentence at Represa. But he is still, perhaps, the most visible, most colorful stadium preacher the NFL has ever seen.

•••

It was a good night for baseball on September 19, 2002 when the Kansas City Royals were playing the Chicago White Sox. In the ninth inning the Royals were up 2 to 1. Their first-base coach, Tom Gamboa, took his position in foul territory and got ready. He never knew what was about to hit him.

Sitting in the stands near Gamboa was William Ligue Jr., age thirty-four. Ligue hadn't been much of a father to his two sons, but on this night he had his fourteen- and fifteen-year-old sons with him to enjoy a Chicago night out at Cominsky Park. Ligue had a troubled past. He had left the boys' mother after being arrested two times for domestic abuse. Maybe to make up for his drug and alcohol abuse and the unstable home life, he would introduce his boys to the Great American pastime.

What Ligue showed his sons was how much he drank. He ordered beer after beer from the vendors and complained of the cost and the slow service. Something ugly was brewing in Ligue's mind. He called his sister and asked her if she was watching the game. She said she wasn't. He told her to turn it on because she would see something on the TV real soon.

Ligue turned and told his sons that Gamboa had laughed at him the whole game and that he saw the coach flip them the bird—shooting his middle finger up. Ligue took his shirt off and handed his younger son his keys and cell phone and asked his older son if he was ready.

The thirty-four-year-old father and his fifteen-year-old progeny jumped out of the stands and ran at Gamboa. The fourteen-year-old Ligue sat in the stands watching his father and older brother jump Gamboa and pummel him into the ground.

"I felt like a football team had hit me from behind. Next thing I knew I'm on the ground trying to defend myself," Gamboa later said of the attack.

The entire Royals dugout ran onto the field to defend their coach. The Royals began to beat the holy hell out of the two Ligues. Security guards ran onto the field and tried to quell the donnybrook, but every time they pulled a Royal off the Ligues another player would jump on. It took ten minutes to end the fight, but security guards finally got the Ligues and the players under control. The guards delivered the Ligues to the Chicago PD, and they were handcuffed and put into police cruisers.

When asked by reporters why he attacked Gamboa, Ligue said, "He got what he deserved."

Ligue told the cops that Gamboa had been mocking him the whole game, making fun of his tattoos and skinny build. Ligue said that when the Royals coach gave him the finger he went wild. Gamboa denied this, and no one backed up Ligue's claim.

After the game, Royals first baseman Mike Sweeney told a reporter, "Security did a good job cleaning it up. If it wasn't for them we'd probably still be beating up on those guys."

Coach Gamboa was given first aid at the stadium for a cut on his forehead but declined further medical aid. He said he had no idea why the Ligues picked him to jump. News clips of the bizarre fight hit every national eleven o'clock news report. William Ligue Jr. became the poster boy for bad fathers.

In August of 2003 in Cook County, Illinois, William Ligue was given thirty months probation. He sneered at reporters outside the courthouse and said, "To me, probation is nothing."

His son, who was never named because of his age, was given five years probation and to this day has stayed out of the police blotter.

But his father wasn't as lucky. In March of 2006—while still on probation—William Ligue Jr. was arrested by the Chicago PD for stealing a car stereo system. It wasn't the theft that angered the judge—it was the high-speed chase through crowded Chicago streets that followed. The judge banged his gavel and sentenced Ligue to his original five-year sentence, and today he sits in the Joliet Prison.

The youngest Ligue boy, Michael the fourteen-year-old who held his father's keys and cell phone in 2002 as Dad and his older brother beat up poor Tom Gamboa, hit the blotter big time in 2007. In March of 2007, Ligue and four friends were arrested for a drive-by shooting in a Chicago neighborhood. A girl had beat up one of Ligue's girlfriends, so they got a car and a gun and shot up the girl's apartment building. Luckily no one was hurt. Ligue sits in prison awaiting trial on firearms charges. He could receive up to fifteen years in jail.

The apple did not fall far from the tree.

•••

Dorian G. Daughtry from East New York in Brooklyn was a promising outfield prospect for the Seattle Mariners in 1987. He could hit, run, throw, and field. But he was a real killer when he had a 9 mm gun in hand.

Daughtry had signed a minor league contract with Seattle and went off to the fresh air of Bellingham, Washington. There he wore the minor league uniform of the Bellingham Mariners, and his roommate was a kid from Donora, Pennsylvania, named Ken Griffey Jr. At twenty years old Daughtry looked like he had it all. But unlike Junior, baseball stardom eluded him.

Daughtry blew out his knee in the minor leagues and had to come back home. In 1987 in the minors Daughtry only managed to hit an anemic .222 with one home run, while Griffey hit a solid .320 and had fourteen home runs.

Three years later on July 22, 1990, any hope for Daughtry ever having a baseball career ended. That night Daughtry's younger brother was involved in a fight with a group of men at a local store in Brooklyn. He reportedly got smacked around and ran out. He went home and came back in a car with his brother Dorian. The brother had a baseball bat and Dorian had a gun.

After a brief and heated argument, according to court records, Dorian Daughtry backed away from the group and pulled his weapon. He fired a few rounds from his 9 mm at the group. One man fired back. Another guy ran off to the other side of the street and also started to shoot at Dorian. Daughtry aimed at this second shooter and let go a hail of bullets. Nine-millimeter shells pinged off the pavement. Yet, not one of the idiots firing weapons was struck by even a single bullet.

The only person hit was nine-year-old Veronica Corales. Her stepfather had double-parked his 1983 Buick LeSabre to drop off his sister-in-law and two children after the family had spent the day at Great Adventure Amusement Park in New Jersey. Veronica was asleep in the car lying next to her mother. One of Daughtry's bullets penetrated the door of the vehicle and struck Veronica in the back of the head. Her father jumped back in the car and rushed to Brookdale Hospital.

Daughtry fled the scene. The men he shot at yelled after him, "You fucked up, Dorian." Everyone on the street knew who did it. They trashed and overturned Daughtry's car, and when he came back to the bodega a few hours later with his sister, who was a cop, he was arrested by the police on the scene for shooting the young girl. His sister knew he would be arrested and convinced Dorian that giving himself up would be the right thing.

The next day's *Daily News* headline was "Stray Shot Hits Girl," with a picture of a pretty and smiling Veronica Corales underneath. On the inside page was a picture of Dorian Daughtry wearing a baseball cap and uniform in happier times. The young girl was on life-support systems and her prognosis didn't look good.

Daughtry pled innocent that night in a Brooklyn court. His lawyer at the time told the media that his client was innocent and that a youth gang named the Wild Pack had shot Corales. No one seemed to know if such a gang existed, but it was a move most lawyers will use when they have nothing else—name unknown assailants to clear your client. A few hours after Dorian Daughtry pled innocent at his arraignment, Veronica Corales died.

Shortly after Daughtry was charged in the 1990 shooting, Ken Griffey Jr. told the *Seattle Times* that he'd been in touch with Daughtry's family. "They say he didn't do it," Griffey said. "I just know he was a great guy and I hate to think of him in trouble."

That week in July of 1990 the police blotter was wild with youths shooting guns. Daughtry's shooting of a child bystander was the first of three such events that would take place that week. The police commissioner, Lee Brown, said he didn't have enough cops to deal with New York's crime problem, and homicide in 1990 was up 20 percent from 1989. Brown told the media that the school system needed to teach kids how to deal with conflict without resorting to violence.

In fact, late July of 1990 was a hot time on the police blotter for all sports. That week the son of Leon Spinks, former heavyweight champion, was shot and killed in East St. Louis, on a bridge leading out of town. Pete Rose was sentenced to five months in prison after pleading guilty to income tax evasion. Commissioner

Fay Vincent issued a lifetime ban to Yankees owner George Steinbrenner for his association with a known gambler.

Prosecutors charged Dorian G. Daughtry with murder in the second degree, and the case went to trial. It was an ugly proceeding, and there was some serious bad blood between the Daughtrys and the relatives of Veronica Corales. Daughtry was found not guilty of the second-degree murder charges but was found guilty, by a jury of his peers in Brooklyn Supreme Court, of manslaughter and reckless endangerment in the first degree. He was sentenced on July 8, 1991, when he was twenty-three, to six to eighteen years for the manslaughter charges and two and a half to seven for the reckless endangerment charges.

Following the trial, Daughtry publicly told the Corales family that he was sorry for Veronica's death. The next day, in Toronto, Daughtry's old minor league roommate, Ken Griffey Jr., went 2-for-3 in the MLB All-Star Game and had broken the record for most votes received.

While a guest of New York State Corrections, Daughtry put down his baseball bat and picked up his jailhouse lawyer pen. He appealed the verdict of judgment, and in 1996 it was overturned on the grounds that improper ex-parte communication had taken place between the judge and jury, among other reasons. There was also talk of the jury being intimidated by courtroom spectators. The Kings County DA's office was astonished by the judge's decision and immediately appealed it to the appellate division.

On May 19, 1997 the original sentence was reinstated and the case was sent back to Kings supreme court for decision on a motion that Daughtry had inadequate counsel. Daughtry remained in Sing Sing while his motion was being decided.

On November 13, 1997 Daughtry was back on Brooklyn soil, this time in handcuffs as he was led into a fifth floor courtroom of the supreme court building on Adams Street. At twenty-nine years old, having served six years of his sentence already, the six-foot, 170-pound Daughtry still looked like a ballplayer.

Just hours before Daughtry's November hearing, his old roommate from the minors, that overachiever named Ken Griffey Jr. of the Seattle Mariners, was named Most Valuable Player of the American League.

Dorian Daughtry lost his appeal in 1998 and was sent back to prison to finish his sentence. He was paroled in 2005 and has led a quiet life since and has stayed off the police blotter, while his former teammate, Ken Griffey, had some hard times with injuries but is still playing some good baseball, now in his hometown of Cincinnati. When Griffey retires he will be a first-ballot winner to get into the Hall of Fame. Maybe Griffey will invite his old minor league mate up to Cooperstown for the induction ceremony. That is, if Daughtry can stay out of the police blotter.

CHAPTER 7

vigilante justice

BACK IN 1978, A NIGHT manager in a McDonald's on Fordham Road in New York's forgotten borough—the Bronx—saw that his district needed a good street cleaning. The neighborhood was turning into a dump, so being a civic-minded youth, he decided to set up a squad of volunteers to sweep up the streets and clean up that part of the Bronx. This gang of happy broom pushers became known as the Rock Brigade—Rock being the night manager's street name. The name he was given by his mama was Curtis Sliwa—founder and still head of the worldwide band of merry crime fighting volunteers called the Guardian Angels. From that broom pushing a career in activism—some might say *vigilantism*—would spring.

The Bronx was spiraling into a disaster during those dark years of the late 1970s and early 1980s. The borough was a symbol for urban blight, a status solidified in the minds of Americans during the 1977 World Series television broadcast from Yankee Stadium. While the Yankees battled the Dodgers on the field, fires were breaking out across the Bronx skyline. The cameras panned the flames engulfing an apartment building as sportscaster Howard Cosell's plaintive wail—"Ladies and gentlemen . . . the Bronx is burning"—pretty much summed up the situation.

But arson and dirty streets weren't the only problems in the Bronx back then. The NYPD faced severe budget problems and had to lay off police officers—this in the middle of a crime wave. The cops that were left were a dispirited bunch.

In those days few city dwellers—not just in New York—even bothered to dial 911 when trouble jumped off. The feeling—right or wrong—was that the cops were too slow to respond and when they did they didn't seem to want to do too much. So a lot of citizens realized that they had to take care of their own problems. A lot of times that backfired. There was a rash of police blotter stories on working stiffs with a weapon still in their hand being gunned down for their paychecks. If you weren't young, strong, or crazy, most times you would rather not come out after dark in American cities in the late 1970s.

To combat this rise in crime Curtis Sliwa took his twelve biggest street sweepers and decided to form a civilian patrol group to fight crime in the streets and subways. They called themselves the Magnificent 13, and on February 13, 1979 they boarded the 4 train—then known as the "Mugger Express"—and began a patrol. The group was looked on with suspicion. It was fine if they wanted to clean up the streets, but a vigilante patrol didn't play as well with regular citizens. It was a little too much like the movie *Death Wish* for most New Yorkers.

A former transit cop who would only use his first name, Phil, said, "Those guys [the Angels] were a joke. Sliwa was in it for the publicity. They caused more harm than good. Half of the Guardian Angels back then were thugs. It was thugs taking on thugs. Sliwa was a pain in the ass. And crime went down in New York well after the Guardian Angels were formed. NYPD was what helped New York's crime wave, not some band of kooks."

Sliwa was making enemies with law enforcement officials and started to make them look bad with his constant running to the press. He made a claim in 1980 that he was kidnapped by transit cops and beaten—or, as he called it, given a "wood shampoo"—because the cops thought that the Guardian Angels were taking jobs away from transit cops. Sliwa showed up at his press conference with his head in bandages, but he had no proof that the cops had beat him.

He was right that cops were wary of the Guardian Angels, and that wariness would prove deadly. In Newark, New Jersey, on December 30, 1981, two Newark cops pulled up to a crime-plagued housing project near Ludlow Street. There was a report of a burglary in progress, and the cops were on edge. It was a dangerous night in one of America's most dangerous cities. The police officers got out of their car with their weapons drawn. Frank Melvin, twenty-six, a Guardian Angel, wearing his red beret and jacket, saw the cops pull up and went to assist them.

Officer Milton Medina didn't see a citizen trying to help: he saw a man running at him and his partner in an aggressive manner. He turned and shot Frank Melvin once through the heart. Melvin never got to see 1982. He would be the first Guardian Angel killed while on patrol.

Sliwa went to Newark and claimed Brown was killed in "cold blood." The cops were investigated, and the Essex County DA claimed the shooting was a "tragic accident" but not a crime.

Sliwa went to war with the New Jersey cops. He hammered them in the press. The cops filed an injunction against Sliwa, and a judge in Newark decreed that Sliwa would have to make a public apology to the cops in Newark for labeling them "racists." Sliwa called a press conference and read the one-page apology in front of Newark cops and the press corps. As soon as he was done, he ripped up the letter and said it was not true, and that he only read it because he was ordered to by a judge. He said he would continue to push to have the cops indicted.

Sliwa was at odds with police everywhere he went. He traveled to Washington, DC, in 1982 to start a new street patrol, but before it began he claimed that the DC cops had grabbed him, thrown him in a car, taken him to a back alley, and beaten him up. There were no witnesses, and no one was ever arrested for these acts. Sliwa came back to New York, and a month later claimed that the New York cops had beaten him. Again, there were no witnesses, and Sliwa was starting to look like the boy who cried wolf. In 1983 a former Guardian Angel went public and said that Sliwa fabricated the police attacks to attract publicity to his organization.

The Guardian Angels' patrols truly angered both cops and criminals, a bad setup from any angle. On July 29, 1983 Juan Oliva and five other Guardian Angels were patrolling in the South Bronx on 170th Street when they got into a fight with a street gang. The Angels were outnumbered and badly beaten. One gang member held Oliva down, and another pumped a bullet into his head. Cops finally came, broke up the fight, and rushed Oliva to a hospital. He lapsed into a coma and finally died months later on Christmas Day 1983.

By the late 1980s the Guardian Angels moved to Times Square to help patrol the troubled theater district. Restaurant and theater owners gave them an office and free food. The NYPD was proving ineffective, and the business owners needed help, so they turned to the Guardian Angels.

Now it is an urban Disneyland, but back then Times Square was a dangerous district full of thieving punks intent on very bad things. Many a night saw the Angels and the local toughs going at it. The cops never seemed to be around when the Angels were in a battle. One night in 1987 a middle-aged couple from Iowa was jumped as they walked to see the play *Cats*. One man held a knife on them as the other robber ripped though their pockets.

Two Guardian Angels turned the corner and saw the muggers. They whistled for backup and took on the thugs. One Angel used a kung-fu kick to knock the knife out of the mugger's hand. The other grabbed the thief with the money and twisted his arm until he let go of it. The Angels handed the tourists their money. The tourists thanked them and scurried off. Other Angels came and held the thieves for the cops. When the cops got there, the thieves claimed that the Angels attacked them. As the tourists—the only other witnesses—were long gone, the cops took both complaints and arrested the Angels and the thugs.

As crime increased in the 1980s, the Guardian Angels came to be more accepted. Local police were having trouble keeping up with crime, and a lot of cities in America welcomed the Angels with open arms. But not everyone was a fan of the Guardian Angels and Curtis Sliwa. By the late 1980s he and his former wife, Lisa, got a gig on WABC radio for a morning talk show. Sliwa took his few hours on the radio in New York to bash then Mafia kingpin John Gotti.

In 1992 John Gotti was on trial in the Eastern District Federal Court, and Sliwa was slamming him daily. In April of 1992 three young hoods met Sliwa outside his apartment as he left to go to work. They threw him to the ground and gave him a beating with baseball bats. Sliwa took a few hard shots but managed to get up and run away. This time the beating was for real, and Sliwa's wrist was broken. The cops were called and did a cursory investigation, but did not apprehend the men who had beaten Sliwa.

To his credit Sliwa stuck to his guns and became even more vehement in his polemics about John Gotti being put away for life. On June 19, 1992 Sliwa hailed a taxi outside his Lower Eastside apartment to go to work. It was early in the morning and still dark out. Sliwa got in and didn't notice that the driver was a young Italian man with a small smile on his face. As the cab turned a corner, another man hiding under the front passenger seat jumped up and fired a gun at Sliwa. Sliwa was hit twice—in the groin and arm. He knew he was trapped and a third bullet was likely to kill him. He jumped at the man in the front seat—knocking him back—and then threw himself out of the window as the cab drove off.

Sliwa survived. Everyone thought Gotti had something to do with it, but no one could prove a thing. As Sliwa was recuperating from his wounds in a hospital, his prayers were answered and John Gotti received life in prison, where he would die in 2002 a broken and bitter man.

Sliwa wanted someone to pay for the hit on him. It took years, but John Gotti Junior was brought to trial on a number of federal racketeering charges—one of them was ordering the hit on Sliwa. Gotti Junior proved elusive. Three times he was put on trial, and three times there was a mistrial. As of 2007 it looks like the feds will not try him again, and still no one has been convicted of shooting Sliwa.

•••

In the 1980s the Guardian Angels were having a psychological impact on people. Taking crime into your own hands suddenly became fashionable. Vigilantism seemed to be the answer. If the cops couldn't do it, someone else would. In 1984 a reed-thin electrical engineer named Bernhard Goetz became so empowered. For awhile he was more famous than the Guardian Angels, and he was proud of the moniker that the tabloids gave him: the Subway Vigilante.

Around 1:30 p.m. on December 22, Goetz, then thirty-seven, entered the number 2 train at 14th Street. It was a Saturday afternoon, and Goetz was meeting some friends at a downtown bar for drinks. He had all of one stop to go.

When he got into the train, four young black men started to eye him up and down, and Goetz got nervous. He was a native New Yorker and was aware of the dangers in New York City during the lawless year of 1984. There were about fifteen other passengers on the train, but the young men seemed intent upon Goetz. They stood in front of him and pushed each other around with some rough horseplay—like they were warming up. Goetz was a streetwise New Yorker who had been mugged three times before, and he felt like this might be the fourth.

The men in front of Goetz were James Ramseur, nineteen, Darrell Cabey, nineteen, Troy Canty, nineteen, and Barry Allen, eighteen.

They had nine convictions and eleven outstanding bench warrants between them. Two of the men—Ramseur and Allen—stood in front of Goetz while Canty told Goetz to give him five dollars. Goetz knew this was no panhandling act.

What the four men did not know was that after Goetz had been mugged the last time in 1982 he took to carrying a five-shot .38 Smith & Wesson revolver. He bought it in the East Village, and then bought other guns in Florida. He had no gun permit but decided the protection was worth the risk. In New York City the Sullivan Law of 1912 decreed a minimum jail time of one year for carrying a concealed weapon. Goetz did not care about that. He had also gone religiously to a shooting range and had become a good shot. This would come in handy.

While the four men leered at him on the subway car, Bernard Goetz stood up and pulled the gun out of his blue windbreaker. With impressive speed and accuracy he let off five shots. The first hit Troy Canty in the chest. The second bullet nailed Barry Allen in the back as he turned to run away. The third shot hit a subway wall and split in half, hitting a woman off to the side—the bullet did not harm her, as it had ricocheted weakly, but the fright of it caused her to faint. The fourth bullet hit Darrell Cabey as he sat and watched in horror. The bullet severed his spinal cord, paralyzing him for life. The irony was that Cabey was probably the only man involved who did not want to mug Goetz. (Months after the incident Allen told cops that they had wanted to mug Goetz and Cabey was the only one not interested in the mugging.)

The fifth bullet nailed James Ramseur in the arm. All four men were on the ground moaning in pain. The emergency brakes had been pulled, and the train came to a screeching halt. Goetz was alleged to have stood over Cabey and said, "You don't look so bad, here's another." It doesn't matter if Goetz said that or not, as he only had five shots and no bullets to reload. Goetz had shot Cabey once and that was enough. With the train stopped a few hundred feet from the Chambers Street Station, the train conductor approached Goetz and asked for the gun.

Goetz decided to run. He exited the train through a rear door, ran down the tunnel, and climbed out at the Chambers Street Station. Goetz later said that if he had waited one more minute the cops would have caught him. As he fled, he heard sirens wailing as the NYPD descended upon the train station. Goetz hailed a yellow cab and went back to his apartment. He grabbed some money, rented a car, and headed north to Vermont.

Six hours later Goetz pulled his car over near a Vermont forest. He walked into the woods well past the tree line and stopped to break his revolver on a rock. He buried the pieces of the gun and then realized he couldn't remember which way he had entered the forest. Later Goetz would tell police he almost died from exposure in the woods that night. He wandered in the freezing cold for two hours still only wearing the thin blue windbreaker he had on when he shot the four men in the subway. He finally found his car and turned on the motor to warm himself up.

Goetz drove to Bennington, Vermont, and took a room in a small bed and breakfast. He was no true fugitive—more a scared little man—but hiding out in a little rural hotel was worthy of a scene in a 1940s film noir.

Back in New York the Goetz shooting spree had set off a media storm. The NYPD sent out an all points bulletin to hunt down the so-called Subway Vigilante. To some in New York—fed up with crime and the NYPD's apparent failure to deal with it—the vigilante was a new kind of folk hero. To others he was a racist targeting innocent young black men. Somewhere in the middle was the truth. Those men—or someone like them—were bound to meet Goetz's gun someday. After a week in Vermont Goetz realized the case was not going to go away.

He drove to a Concord, New Hampshire, police station and surrendered himself to Officer Dan Foote. At first Foote thought that Goetz was an EDP—an emotionally disturbed person. Goetz talked with Foote for more than four hours, and the cop gradually realized that this was the real deal. Officer Foote put in a call to the NYPD. The police department sent up a team of detectives, but a few top brass went with them because the higher-ups knew the detectives were on Goetz's side and would tell him if he just kept his mouth shut he would likely get off on any charges. The cops knew that the young men who had been shoot by Goetz were well on their way to being career criminals and figured they got what they deserved. The bosses made sure the cops never got the chance to give Goetz that advice on silence. If he kept his mouth shut, public opinion was likely to lean in his favor. But Goetz was a talker and a bit of a nut, and when he got to talking, he sounded like a loon.

Goetz's arraignment back in a New York court attracted hordes of press and spectators. Goetz was freed on bail on gun and assault charges, and he may have walked on all of those charges had he kept his mouth shut as the cops would have advised. According to police sources the Manhattan DA was thinking about giving Goetz probation on just the gun charges, but then he gave interview after interview to TV and newspaper reporters about how good he felt shooting the young men. Goetz's big mouth—cops working the case agreed—got him charged with the more serious attempted murder charges. Most people could understand Goetz doing what he did; it was the lack of remorse that gave people pause.

Goetz had no money for a lawyer, so the Guardian Angels took up a collection in the subway system to raise money for his legal defense. Commuters sick of roving packs of feral youths gladly gave up the money. The plus side to Goetz's attack was that subway crime was down the first six months after the shooting.

When Goetz went to trial, it was a media circus. It took a month to assemble a jury. Out of the four hundred jurors called, more than half had also been victims of a mugger and thus could not serve.

In 1987 the jury found Goetz not guilty on seventeen counts of attempted murder and assault. He was only found guilty of illegally possessing a handgun. Goetz served eight and a half months in Rikers Island prison and has since led a law-abiding life. Barry Allen, James Ramseur, and Troy Canty went on to further their criminal careers with arrests, convictions, and jail time. Darrell Cabey remained paralyzed but won a $43 million lawsuit against Goetz. Goetz had no money, so as of 2007 Cabey has collected next to nothing on the judgment.

In 2002 Goetz ran for office in New York as the public advocate. He lost and has since tried to bring media attention to his views on vegetarianism and his love of urban squirrels. His shooting spree got more coverage. Goetz is clearly an odd fellow, and he will not discuss whether he still carries a gun, but he has never been mugged after the 1984 shooting. Maybe that's because of what he said in a recent interview: "I would, without any hesitation, shoot a violent criminal again."

•••

Another man was attacked in June of 2006 by a crew of wild teenagers in Atlanta, Georgia. He became a hero in the south, and he was the anti-Goetz.

Thomas Autry, thirty-six, was a former cook in the Marine Corps who was working as a waiter at a restaurant in Atlanta. He made all of $80 a week plus tips. He was walking from work to his girlfriend's house on a hot night around midnight when a Cadillac pulled over and five teenagers jumped out, demanding Autry's money.

Autry is a big and gentle man. He is in good shape and he stands six-foot-six, so one has to wonder just what these teen thugs were thinking. They formed a semicircle around Autry, and one pointed a shotgun at him while another had a .380 pistol. Autry kicked the shotgun out of the kid's hands and ran off. The teenagers chased him down and cornered him near an alley. The pack of teens consisted of four boys and one girl. The girl was the wildest of the bunch.

She had brass knuckles on and was beating Autry's chest. Another kid hit him with the .380 on the head. Autry was taking a pounding, but started to fight back.

"I was going to survive. It was either me or them, and I choose me in that equation," Autry told a local Atlanta reporter.

His military training kicked in. Autry pulled out a box cutter he was carrying and started to slash out at the teens. Incredibly, the teens never fired their weapons. Autry did some damage. Two of the teens were badly hurt. The four boys limped back to their car carrying the girl. They started up the Caddy and peeled out. Autry ran to a phone booth and called the Atlanta PD with a plate number and a solid description of his attackers.

The five teens were caught by the police at a local hospital. Amy Martin, seventeen, was the girl who attacked Autry. She was pronounced dead at the hospital from stab wounds. Chris Daniels, eighteen, was admitted in critical condition. The cops charged Daniels and the three other boys with armed robbery. It seemed that Thomas Autry was not their first victim. The cops had been looking for this crew of cruising muggers.

"These are the individuals we have been looking for during the past two nights. They've been driving around . . . robbing people," Atlanta detective Danny Stephens told the *Atlanta Constitution*.

When the news broke of Autry's brave act, he became an instant local hero. The police pressed no charges against him and no one cared that he'd killed a girl. No one except Autry. "I was trying to protect myself," he said. "I'm sorry. . . . They tried to rob me for eight dollars and that is the thing that is going to haunt me for the rest of my life. Somebody lost their life through my hands for eight dollars."

Autry was offered jobs and money for his counterattack on the teens, but he remained contrite and derived no pleasure from the fact that he had to take a life in order to survive. He remained the reluctant vigilante.

•••

Another vigilante operated out of Bellingham, Washington, and his mission was pure revenge. That city started a Web site that listed all of the level III sexual predators living in the community and providing their names, addresses, ages, and offenses. Level III offenders—deemed so by the court after trial—are the most serious of sexual predators, and when they were released into the community, law enforcement tries their best to keep a short list on them. No one in law enforcement realized that the Web site was a green light for vigilantes to hunt down these loathed predators.

One night in August of 2005 a man posing as an FBI agent knocked on the door of a boardinghouse where three level III sexual predators lived. The man claimed he was there to warn them of a plot hatched on the Internet to kill them. One of the men, James Russell, took the information and had to excuse himself to go to work. He left the agent and two of his roommates, Hank Eisses, forty-nine, and Victor Vasquez, sixty-eight, standing at the door.

When Russell returned to the house in the morning, he found Eisses and Vasquez dead on the floor. They had both been shot in the head. Russell called the cops and told them of the FBI man's visit. The Washington State FBI office had no record of any agent going to the house to warn of an assassination attempt.

The local police were not convinced that the Web site led to the killing, but allowed that it might have been used by the killer. Eisses and Vasquez—while having once committed heinous acts against minors—were now on the straight and narrow path and led quiet, law-abiding lives. But their past may have come out of the dark to haunt them.

A week later the Bellingham PD found a blog posted in an America Online journal written by someone calling himself Agent Life and boasting of killing the two pedophiles. He claimed that with child molesters, it was one strike and you are out.

The blog entry read, "I am Agent Life! And I alone am responsible for the deaths of the two level three pedophiles in Bellingham, Washington, and they are not to be the last to be executed unless things change for the better."

The police traced the journal to a huge man named Mike Mullen, and on Labor Day 2005 he was arrested for the killings. He confessed to the police that he killed the two men because they were pedophiles. He had been molested as a child and he wanted revenge on all perverts.

In December of 2005, while Mullen was sitting in jail unable to make his $1 million bail, another vigilante killer picked up his torch. James Garret, sixty-three, a level III sexual offender, was killed in his house on South 18th Street in Yakima, Washington. The Yakima PD reported that Garret died from one gunshot to the chest. They had no leads, and the killer remains at large.

Mike Mullen pled guilty in his case, and was sentenced in March of 2006 to forty-four years in a Washington State prison.

•••

There are times when vigilantes can be wrong—dead wrong. A popular young man in Marshville, North Carolina, went missing in September of 2006. A posse of his friends and family got together to search for the missing man—Patrick McClendon.

McClendon was well loved by his neighbors and the children in Marshville. He always had a smile and a greeting for everyone. When he took his car out to go to the grocery store and never returned, his friends and family became concerned. By the fourth day, they turned frantic.

Tony Blakeney found McClendon's car hidden in the woods on his property. He called 911, and he told McClendon's family and friends what he had found. That was a big mistake. The friends turned on Blakeney and beat him senseless, convinced that he knew what had become of McClendon.

A detective from the Marshville PD arrived, and the crowd turned their fury on him. He had to call for backup, and when the other cops arrived, the crowd ran off. Tony Blakeney had been beaten to death.

Later in the week the Marshville PD arrested Leonard Staton, eighteen, for the murder of Patrick McClendon. The body was found in the woods not far from where McClendon's car was dumped. He had been dead for four days when he was found, killed by a gunshot to the head. Tony Blakeney was also dead, and he had had nothing to do with the crime.

"Tony Blakeney was an innocent man," Deputy Chief Ben Bailey told a local reporter. "This is a prime example of what happens when people take matters into their own hands and don't let the criminal justice system do its work."

Eleven men were arrested for Blakeney's death, and when they were being led to jail, they were told it was Leonard Staton who had killed their friend. Staton had been in the crowd when Blakeney was beaten to death. The eleven men face murder charges for Blakeney's death, and their former friend, Staton, is up on murder charges for killing McClendon.

•••

Sometimes cops can take the law into their own hands and act with a vigilante-like vengeance. On September 28, 2006, Angilo Freeland was driving his car in Lakeland, Florida, when Deputy Doug Speirs pulled him over for speeding. Speirs asked Freeland for his license, and he produced a fake-looking Florida State ID. Freeland asked the cop, "Will I go to jail for not having a license?"

Before the deputy could answer, Freeland went running into the nearby woods. Speirs called for backup, and Deputy Matt Williams pulled up with his trained police dog, Dioggi. The two cops and the dog scoured the woods for Freeland.

As Williams approached a brushy area, Freeland jumped out and shot and killed the police dog. Before Williams could return fire, Freeland hit him with a fusillade of bullets, knocking him to the ground. Freeland then stood over the deputy and put two bullets in his head, killing him.

Speirs heard the gunfire and called to Williams on the radio that he was coming. As Williams was dead, all this accomplished was to alert Freeland. Freeland hid behind a ridge, popped out as Speirs approached, and shot him once in the leg. The deputy returned fire but missed. Freeland ran into the woods, and Speirs called for more backup.

This set off one of the biggest manhunts in the history of Polk County, Florida. More than five hundred cops joined in the pursuit of Freeland through the woods. Sheriff Grady Judd warned, "We're prepared for a gunfight, if he wants a gunfight."

Boy, were they ever ready. The next morning a team of ten SWAT cops found Angilo Freeland hiding under a fallen oak tree with Deputy Williams's .45 in his hand. That was all the proof they needed. No one tried to arrest Freeland. The cops claimed he raised his weapon, and they squeezed off 110 rounds, hitting Freeland with 68 bullets and killing him.

A local reporter asked the sheriff whether all that firepower was necessary for one man. Sheriff Judd answered, "I suspect the only reason 110 rounds were all that was fired was that's all the ammunition they had. We're not going to take a chance of him shooting back. . . . God will be the judge and jury this time. The killer chose his end. He raised his hand, and it had a firearm in it. That was the last thing he ever did."

Some of the citizens of Polk County had a problem with the excessive force used on Angilo Freeland and the vigilante bluster of Sheriff Judd. It was like he was some Wild West marshall stringing up the bad guys. Others thought that a man who had just executed a cop with two bullets in the head got what he deserved. Pressure was put on Governor Jeb Bush to investigate the shooting. The investigation ended in March of 2007 with no charges being brought against the police.

Freeland's family argued that he was shot so many times because Freeland was a black man. The family claimed he had no criminal record. A check on Angilo Freeland showed he had an extensive criminal record and he had a cache of weapons and drugs in his house.

•••

Vigilantes can be found in the strangest places. Even the seemingly peaceful Canadian fishing island—Grand Manan—has seen a wild case of islanders taking the law into their own hands.

This all began when a thin and surly man, Ron Ross, moved onto Grand Manan Island in 2006. Ross, forty-three, grew up in nearby Nova Scotia but spent a lot of time on Grand Manan working on lobster boats. Grand Manan is a sleepy island village located in the Bay of Fundy. The only way on and off the island is a twenty-mile ferry ride to the nearest city—St. Johns. Ross seemed to like that the island was cut off from the rest of civilization. He enjoyed the life of freedom that the island afforded him, and he also appreciated that a man could be left alone.

Ross liked to drink and play loud music. Real loud. And he would turn his speakers toward the street so his neighbors could hear his music selections. He opened his house to a group of surly-looking misfits from the mainland, and the parties would go on and on. Rumors flew around the island that Ross was dealing crack out of his house. The 2,500 residents of the seventeen-mile-long island became convinced that Ross was a bad man and had to go.

Laura Buckley, an innkeeper, told *The New Yorker* magazine that Ross "had asshole issues that were much larger than being a drug dealer."

The alleged crack dealing was what bothered residents the most. Ross's house was on a block full of children, and he was deemed an unfit neighbor. The folks of Grand Manan had fairly liberal attitudes toward drug use when it came to marijuana. The island had little to do in the way of entertainment for young people, and drinking and light drug use were an accepted option. The island had very little funding for police and there were only four Royal Canadian Mounted Police (RCMP) assigned there. There was no money for drug-sniffing dogs on the ferry, so getting illegal drugs on the island was very easy. As long as it was amongst the natives and no one got crazy, some drug use was cool. It was a common sight to see a fisherman smoking a joint or a hash pipe. Even cocaine use might be pardoned. But crack? No! And an outsider dealing crack? Absolutely not.

Carter Foster, a big and strong fisherman, lived across the street from Ross and soon became his bête noire. The two men eyed each other suspiciously whenever they came out of their houses. Foster told the RCMP his suspicion that Ross was dealing crack, and the police got a search warrant and tossed Ross's house. The police found no drugs. Ross stood in his driveway smirking at his neighbors.

In June of 2006 a number of residents reported that their homes and cars were being burglarized. Power tools were stolen at an alarming clip, and the island scuttlebutt became that Ross was accepting stolen goods as payment for crack. Never mind that there was no proof Ross dealt drugs—a rumor on an island like Grand Manan took on the cloak of truth.

The islanders were convinced that a GMC truck in Ross's driveway was being used to steal the power tools. On the night of July 4, the truck was set on fire and destroyed. Ross ran around the island screaming for revenge. He told some residents that they had better start sleeping with one eye open because he was going to burn their homes down.

The police never did find who burned the truck in Ross's driveway, and the tensions between Ross and the islanders kept growing.

On July 21 a rumor circulated around Grand Manan that Ross had hired a group of Hell's Angels and they were coming out on the ferry to burn down some homes on the island.

A group of thirty men congregated on Carter Foster's lawn and stood cursing at Ross's house. Some of the men had just come from a baseball game and were holding wooden bats. The RCMP knew this could get bad, so an officer was dispatched to Foster's home and he told the men that the rumor was false. There were no evil strangers on the ferry, and there were only ten people at Ross's house.

The cop left, and Ross and his friends came out of the house cursing at Foster and his crew. Foster and Ross went at it, and Foster, being the bigger man, started giving Ross a beating, telling him to move off the island. As Foster got Ross into a headlock, someone in Ross's crew fired a gun.

Foster and his friends ran back to their yard and took cover. Foster bolted into his house and came out on his roof with a rifle. He proceeded to shoot up a truck parked in Ross's driveway. Foster later told cops he wasn't shooting at humans but rather just the truck to disable it in case Ross decided to drive it to burn down homes.

Ross's friends returned gunfire, and for twenty minutes bullets were popping on the island. Incredibly, no one was hit with a single shot. The RCMP came by, but everyone ran away. When the cops left, they came back, and the fights started again. Ross was beaten up by a few men while two others snuck around the rear of the house and set Ross's back wall on fire.

The volunteer fire company of Grand Manan responded. Rocks were thrown at them as they put out the fire. The RCMP knew this was not going to get better, so they escorted Ross and his friends away from the house.

At 5:00 a.m. as the house stood empty, a huge explosion was heard in the house, and flames again shot up the walls. When the firemen showed up, trucks parked in front of the house to block them. The trucks were removed, but then the firefighters had to deal with six islanders linking their arms and blocking the fire truck from getting near the fire. By the time they were able to put the fire out, Ross's house had burned to the ground. It was completely destroyed.

When news of this broke the next day the Canadian media was appalled by the mob rule on Grand Manan. Editorials were written that vigilantism would not be tolerated in Canada. The RCMP arrested two men from Foster's crew on arson charges for the earlier fire, and Foster and two others were arrested for illegal use of a firearm for the shooting incidents. No one was ever charged with burning Ross's house down. Ross was also arrested for illegal use of a firearm and for threatening residents with arson.

Ten days after this crazed mob took over Grand Manan, a new rumor spread around the island that another house suspected of being a crack den was going to be burned down. The RCMP had had enough and sent out seventy officers to quell any more vigilante attacks or arson.

The next day the islanders howled about the RCMP spending $100,000 for one night, and yet they couldn't afford one drug-sniffing dog on the ferry. The mayor of Grand Manan called for an investigation into the RCMP for wasting so much money. The cops can't win for losing on Grand Manan.

The island quieted down, and the locals rallied around the five men who had been arrested for attacking Ross and burning down his house. The feeling was that they did what the RCMP wouldn't or couldn't do—get Ross off their island. Banners were hung on the Grand Manan ferry with the legend, "Free Our Heroes." A newspaper poll showed that 82 percent felt that their "boys" should not be tried for any crime.

The trial began in November of 2006, and the two men charged with firearms violations were found not guilty. Carter Foster was found guilty of illegal use of a firearm, and the two men charged with arson were also found guilty. The islanders protested, but at the sentencing a week later they were happy. The harshest sentence was that the men had been under house arrest, which would suffice as time served.

Ron Ross remained under house arrest at his father's home in New Brunswick. He was not allowed on Grand Manan Island. His trial began in April of 2007, and he was found not guilty of the gun charges. The judge felt that the crew at Foster's house meant to harm Ross and he was in his rights to shoot at them. He was found guilty on the charges of making deadly threats, and he was sentenced to time served.

Ross remains in New Brunswick, and the restrictions of his probation require that he stay away from Grand Manan Island. He told local reporters that when his probation ends in two years, he might just move back to Grand Manan.

Foster and the other islanders will be waiting for Ross if he ever does come back on the ferry. This could be a modern-day, long-running feud like the old Hatfields and McCoys.

•••

One of the wilder groups to take justice into the streets was the Jewish Defense League (JDL), started by a rabbi, Meir Kahane, in the lawless days of 1968. Kahane was appalled that many elderly Jews living in the ghetto were being targeted for mugging and beatings by black criminals. Kahane saw that the NYPD was not helping out the older Jewish population in New York, so he banded together a bunch of young and wild Jewish men to go out and avenge their elders. The JDL motto back then was, "Every Jew a .22!"

Elderly Jews were escorted around the neighborhoods by JDL toughs, and the tension between the blacks and the Jews led to quite a few fights. The JDL used whistles to communicate, and if they were getting the worst of the battle, they would whistle for backup. The sound of whistles blowing in the ghetto caused blacks and Jews to come running. Neither side was willing to call the cops.

On February 29, 1972, Kahane spoke at City College about Jews defending themselves. Some students on the campus took offense at what Kahane was saying and tried to storm the stage. Kahane's JDL fellows leapt into action. They were ready for a rumble. They picked up the sticks they had brought with them and proceeded to beat the holy hell out of the college kids. Kahane smiled from the podium and jumped into the fray when the NYPD showed up.

It was an old-fashioned donnybrook, and dozens of JDL members—including Kahane—and scores of college kids were arrested. The cops threw them into holding cells at Midtown North, and the fights broke out again. The cops let them battle it out in the cells until they all ran out of steam.

The NYPD marked the JDL as a group to keep a close watch on, much like the Black Panthers. They would regularly raid JDL meetings and haul in the members for disturbing the peace. As the JDL members would not go gently into the night, charges of resisting arrest would also be added.

Some sadistic NYPD officers would put lone JDL members in holding cells full of blacks and then announce that the man was a member of the JDL. The blacks knew what that meant, and the cops would walk away laughing as the JDL member was attacked.

Kahane grew tired of being harassed in New York and made plans to head to the land of milk and honey—Israel. He moved to Israel in the late 1970s and toured the country making incendiary speeches, calling for Jews to kill and destroy all members of the Palestine Liberation Organization (PLO). He denounced Islam and Palestine and wanted Israel to become a military state to protect itself. He had followers and was elected to the Knesset (Israeli legislature), but the Israeli leaders felt he was a danger to a civilized society and had him deported back to America in 1985. He was banned from Israel for life.

Kahane was allowed back into America because by then the JDL furor had died down and Kahane was a forgotten man in America. He came back to his hometown in New York and continued his JDL rants. He had fewer followers, but those who remained were loyal to him. The NYPD didn't even bother to keep tabs on Kahane. They considered him to be old news.

Not everyone forgot about Kahane. By 1990 Kahane knew he was being targeted by a group of radical Muslims in Brooklyn. The JDL took him seriously, but when they reported it to the NYPD, the cops ignored them. The JDL had no real proof, and the cops thought a bunch of Muslims in Brooklyn were no big threat—at least not to anyone not named Kahane. That proved a major and fatal mistake, and this group would go on to do some terrible deeds in the city, but in 1990 Kahane was their target.

On November 5, 1990, Kahane gave a speech at the Marriot East Side hotel. The hall was packed with his followers. Many in the crowd took note of a chubby man in the back. He was a stranger, but they assumed he was a new convert. The man was El Sayyid Nosair, and he was about to meet Kahane. As Kahane's speech wound down, Nosair approached the stage and pulled out a .357 Magnum and fired once. The bullet tore through Kahane's neck, killing him. The hall erupted, and Nosair fought his way through the crowd by swinging his gun at JDL members. He made it to the door, but there he was grabbed by Irving Franklin.

Franklin was seventy-three, but he would not let go of Nosair. Nosair punched and kicked the old man, but Franklin hung onto his leg like a hungry dog with a bone. Nosair shot him in the leg and finally escaped.

At this moment, Nosair and his two confederates outside turned the episode into a Keystone Kops caper. Nosair saw a livery cab outside the hotel and jumped in, assuming it was the getaway car. It wasn't. The driver of Nosair's getaway car was still searching for a parking spot, and the lookout man outside the hotel had wandered off to get something to eat.

When Nosair saw a frightened cab driver whom he didn't recognize, he realized he was in trouble. He put his gun to the taxi driver's head and demanded that he drive away. Fast. A Kahane follower jumped on the cab's hood and tried to break the windshield. The cabbie pulled into traffic and then slammed on the brakes. The driver ran off into the night, leaving Nosair alone in the cab.

Nosair jumped out of the cab and ran, chased by a mob of angry Kahane supporters. As Nosair turned a corner, he came face to face with a uniformed postal police officer. Nosair fired at the cop and missed, and the postal cop fired once, hitting Nosair in the neck and knocking him down. NYPD officers finally reached Nosair, put him in cuffs, and took him to the hospital. Given all the witnesses, and the quick apprehension of the shooter, this should have been an open-and-shut homicide case. But it got strange. The NYPD raided Nosair's home in Cliffside, New Jersey, and confiscated dozens of boxes with detailed plans of the hit and other terrorist plots and dreams. They did nothing with this other than hand it over to the FBI, where apparently nothing further happened with it, with chilling ramifications.

Kahane had no friends at the NYPD, and the mood over his death was, in the words of one cop who worked the case, that "those who live by the sword die by the sword." The NYPD put out an official statement that the Kahane shooting was a random act of violence by a man that the cops assumed had a grudge against Kahane.

A year and a month after the shooting, a jury found Nosair not guilty of murder. Many critics of the case said the fact that the jury discounted the numerous eyewitnesses indicated how much those twelve people disliked Kahane. Many African-American New Yorkers did hold a grudge against Kahane and the JDL, as they felt that the JDL was a racist organization and their leader got what he deserved.

The jury did find Nosair guilty of second-degree assault and weapons charges, and he went to Attica for a twenty-year stint. But the case did not end there. In February of 1993 when a bomb went off in the World Trade Center parking lot and six innocent people were killed, reports surfaced that the boxes found in Nosair's house in New Jersey in 1990 had contained extensive plans on how to plant such a bomb in the World Trade Center.

Sheik Omar Abdul Rahman and eleven others—including Nosair—went on trial for the World Trade Center bombing. The FBI took them by helicopter from a Brooklyn federal jail to a Manhattan federal courthouse. The FBI had the Muslims wear hoods over their heads so they could not get a bird's-eye view of the city they had tried to destroy. One agent couldn't help himself. As the helicopter flew near the World Trade Center, he took the hood off of Sheik Omar Abdul Rahman, pointed to the Twin Towers, and said, "Well, Sheik, it looks like they are still standing."

Rahman smiled at the agent and said, "Not for long."

The FBI had a good laugh at the Sheik's boasting. They knew they had an open-and-shut case, and these Muslim whack jobs would be put away for a very long time. They thought they had solved the problem of terrorist attacks.

The twelve were all found guilty, and Nosair was tried in federal court for Kahane's killing. This time he was found guilty and was given a life sentence. All of the terrorists from that 1993 bombing received lifetime sentences, and today they remain in maximum-security federal prisons.

That the FBI and NYPD never translated the evidence from Nosair's original case was just pure malfeasance. The whole thing was covered up, and no one in law enforcement was ever disciplined over this deadly snafu.

In 2006 an Israeli newspaper reported that former detective John Molehill—who worked the 1990 Kahane case—admitted that the NYPD really fouled up, and that the Nosair materials they seized in 1990 had attack plans for the World Trade Center, the Empire State Building, and the Statue of Liberty.

The violence would continue for the Kahane family. On December 31, 2000, Binyamin Kahane—Meir Kahane's son—was killed along with his wife in Israel during a roadside machine-gun attack. A Palestinian group called the Intifada Martyrs took credit for the attack.

The Martyrs might have taken a page out of Meir Kahane's own playbook. Kahane was once quoted as saying, "No trait is more justified than revenge in the right time and place."

CHAPTER

8

are these the real Sopranos?

ON MARCH 3, 1999 TWO members of the New Jersey–based crime family known as the DeCavalcantes were secretly taped by FBI agents assigned to the organized crime division. The taping was done during their car ride into New York City for a sit-down with some big city mafioso. The audio reveals Joseph "Tin Ear" Scalfani and Anthony Rotundo discussing what was then a new mob show on HBO.

Scalfani: "Hey, what's this fucking thing, *Sopranos*. What the fuck are they? Is that supposed to be us?"

Rotundo: "You are in there; they mention your name in there."

Scalfani: "What did they say?"

Rotunda: "Watch out for that guy. . . . Every show you watch more and more you pick up somebody. Every show."

Scalfani: "Yeah, but it's not me, I'm not even existing over there."

Rotunda: "One week it was Corky, one week it was the guy that died and had stomach cancer. . . . What characters. Great acting."

The DeCavalcante family had operated under the shadows of their more glamorous and well known Mafia cousins in New York.

But in 1999 with the rise of the hit series, *The Sopranos*, the DeCavalcante family felt they had finally hit the big time. But for years some mob-beat writers and members of the New York Mafia claimed that the DeCavalcantes were a joke—a mere half of a family.

"That is incorrect. They are a real family. They're not some mere minor league outfit," Jerry Capeci said when asked to discuss the DeCavalcantes.

Capeci is one of America's foremost experts on the American Mafia and has his own Web site dedicated to it at www.ganglandnews.com. Capeci always knew that the Mafia was gold on the police blotter. After a successful stint as the *Daily News* mob reporter—and three best-selling books—he now works as director of public relations for John Jay College in New York City.

"The DeCavalcantes are a legitimate mob family. They are just not as powerful as the five New York families. The problem between them and the New York families is that the New York guys felt that the DeCavalcantes were making guys who were not up to snuff. The talent pool in New Jersey seemed watered down to the New York crew. They looked at them like they were a bit soft."

Capeci thinks that the DeCavalcantes' lower profile helped them stay out of trouble in the 1980s and early '90s as the New York families were systematically taken apart by the FBI.

"I think they just slipped through the cracks. Mafioso families are all pretty much the same. Same structure, same mentality. Make as much money as you can without getting caught, no matter who you may hurt in the process."

Why did the New York mobsters think that the Jersey mobsters were weak? Was it a case of the suburbs not producing good criminals?

"It's a case of taking whatever you can get," Capeci said.

•••

Before the 1999 debut of *The Sopranos* and the airing of the DeCavalcante tapes, not many people knew of the family. But law enforcement officials in New Jersey knew that they had been around for years working their illicit crafts in and around Elizabeth, New Jersey.

The first recorded history of the DeCavalcantes was in the early 1960s when the New Jersey State Organized Crime Task Force taped the long laments of a man known as Simone "Sam the Plumber" DeCavalcante. He was called Sam the Plumber because one of his legitimate jobs was in plumbing supply. Sam the Plumber was the head of the little-known Jersey family named after him—the DeCavalcantes. He held court in his Kenilworth, New Jersey, office while the cops listened in.

"We got thirty-one or thirty-two soldiers," said DeCavalcante. "Most of them are old people who ain't making much money. . . . If I can continue for two or three years I will be able to show forty thousand or fifty thousand dollars legitimately and can walk out. Then my family situation can be resolved."

Sam the Plumber was able to realize those simple dreams, and in 1973 he retired from mob life and moved to Florida. This alone made New York suspicious, because not many Mafia bosses get out alive and unindicted.

Sam DeCavalcante lived for twenty-four law-abiding years in Florida. He died there in 1997 a free and happy man. His mob family up north continued on without him, and as they stayed under the radar of law enforcement, they were able to flourish in the backwaters of New Jersey. They were involved in waste removal, gambling, rigged construction bids, protection rackets, prostitution, truck hijacking, and drug dealing. They had a whole state to work in, and not much law enforcement interference, while the New York boys were under constant surveillance in the city.

But the DeCavalcantes got no respect. New York mobsters through the years have derided Jersey mob guys as " farmers," and the late John Gotti went so far as to announce an edict that any New

York mobster who got made in Jersey would not be recognized as "a friend of ours." The New York Mafia believed that mob washouts in New York were fleeing to Jersey to get made because of the reduced wise-guy competition in the Garden State.

The respect that the DeCavalcantes longed for took a real hit with the rise of John D'Amato. In 1990 when John Riggi—then boss of the DeCavalcante family—was jailed, he made John D'Amato acting boss because of D'Amato's close ties to John Gotti. Gotti had invited D'Amato to his son's wedding, and D'Amato was also a regular visitor to Gotti's social clubs.

What wasn't known to the DeCavalcantes was that D'Amato was gay. He frequented many gay clubs in New York and kept a boyfriend hidden in a getaway apartment. When whispers about D'Amato's sexuality got out, the Jersey mob knew it had to do something quick. In the hyper-macho world of organized crime, a gay acting boss would be a permanent joke at the expense of the New Jersey mob. To their minds, there was only one thing they could do. D'Amato had to be whacked.

In 1992 DeCavalcante captains held a secret meeting, and Anthony Capo was given the task of making the hit on D'Amato. He and another man picked D'Amato up and were supposedly driving him to a meeting with other members of the family. As they bantered in the car, Capo sat in the backseat and took out his handgun. He shot D'Amato four times in the head, and then they drove the body to a safe house for disposal.

D'Amato's body was never found. When Anthony Capo flipped for the feds and turned state's evidence in 1998 and the whole story on D'Amato came out, many a New York mobster sat in a jail cell convinced that his suspicions of the DeCavalcantes were justified.

The last great time for DeCavalcantes was in the early 1990s, when federal law enforcement was too busy with Racketeer Influenced and Corrupt Organization Act (RICO) cases on John Gotti's family to be bothered with the mob in New Jersey. Local cops can only do so much damage to a Mafia family. The NYPD went head to head with the Mafia for years, and it was only when the FBI got involved that the Mafia was finally taken out. In New Jersey the local and state cops did some fine work on the DeCavalcantes, but it was a case-by-case war and never against the whole family.

•••

Was *The Sopranos* based on the DeCavalcante family? HBO has now cancelled the series, but A&E has picked it up in syndication, and the show will be with us for a very long time. There are many connections between the show and the real New Jersey mob. Both had involvement in Wall Street, working "pump-and-dump" schemes on unsuspecting stock traders. Both dealt heavily in stolen goods and even moved into collectibles, stealing rare comic books and the screenplay for *The Wizard of Oz*.

Both families hail from New Jersey and—according to the FBI tapes—the DeCavalcantes swore that someone from *The Sopranos* had to have been tracking them. That may be just some vain thinking, as mobsters love to see themselves portrayed in the media.

"I don't think the *Sopranos* were based on the DeCavalcante family, per se," Jerry Capeci said. "The show is more of a montage of known mobster idiosyncrasies pulled from various sources to come up with enough interesting characters to make a nice show."

The Sopranos filmed many scenes in real-life settings in New Jersey. The following locations were used on the show, and can be visited by tourists:

1. The Bada Bing is a real strip club on Route 17 South in Lodi, New Jersey. It's actually called Satin Dolls, but the dancers seen on some of *The Sopranos* episodes do perform there.
2. Also on Route 17 is Ramsey Outdoors, the sporting goods

store that the Sopranos took over when the degenerate gambler Davey Scatino—played by Robert Patrick, whose best turn as an actor was as a cyborg cop in *Terminator 2*—got so far in debt he had to give up his store to pay off his gambling losses. After that episode, the owners of the real-life Ramsey Outdoors had to put a sign up indicating that they were still open, and that *The Sopranos* is fiction.

3. Tony Soprano's McMansion, where he feeds his ducks and fights with Carmella, is high in the hills of North Caldwell near Mountain Avenue.
4. Pizzaland, seen on the opening credits of *The Sopranos*, is located on Route 7 West by Ridge Road.
5. Fountains of Wayne is located in Wayne, New Jersey. The store is where a cop—played by convicted murderer and star of the 1990's WB TV show *Roc* Charles Dutton—works off-duty and turns down a bribe by Tony Soprano.
6. Satriale's Pork Store, where the boys sit outside, and sometimes go in to make a little sausage out of their victims, is located at 101 Kearney Avenue in Kearney. The store is abandoned when *The Sopranos* aren't in town.
7. Livia Soprano's house is located at 55 Gould Street in Verona, New Jersey.

Below are some *Sopranos* characters, and their parallels in the real-life DeCavalcante crime family:

VITO SPATOFORE/JOHN D'AMATO

Joseph Gannascoli played gangster Vito Spatafore, the gay, closeted member of the Soprano family. The character seems directly based on the real-life gay mafioso, John D'Amato. They both meet similar ends. In *The Sopranos*, Spatafore was whacked by the New York crew because they believed his homosexuality brought shame on the Mafia. D'Amato was hit by his own family for the same reasons. Both were big earners and good mobsters, but their sexuality could not be tolerated in that arcane setting.

HESH RABKIN/CORKY VASTOLA

Jerry Adler plays Hesh Rabkin on *The Sopranos*. He is an elder, all-knowing Jewish mobster, who early on forged a career in the music business. In real life, Gaetano "Corky" Vastola—while not Jewish—also had a long and fruitful career in the music business. On the 1999 FBI tape, "Corky" is mentioned as being one of the characters on the show. Vastola was part of the DeCavalcante family from 1960 to 1998 and is best known for dealing one of the hardest and most infamous Mafia blows to the music industry.

On *The Sopranos*, Hesh has an office full of gold records on the walls from an R&B label he owned years earlier. Hesh had given a lot of young blacks a start in the music business, but he kept all the author's rights to the songs and was still making money from them.

In one episode, a hip-hop artist named Massive G, played by Bokeem Woodbine, tries to strong-arm Hesh into giving his distant cousin $400,000 for back royalties for the songs Hesh owns. In a face-off, Massive G asks what part of the songs Hesh wrote. Hesh hems and haws and then answers that back then music was made in a collaborative effort. Massive G threatens legal action, but Hesh is one smart man. He tells Massive G that his rap records contain many samples of songs Hesh owns, and he will sue Massive G if he continues his court action against Hesh. Both men drop the cases, and peace is restored.

If only real life was as neat. Corky Vastola was an active mob member in New Jersey, but he also promoted concerts and was part owner of Roulette Records and was listed as a cowriter on a few hit records, such as the Cleftones' "You Baby You" and the Wrens' "Hey Girl." There is no report of an old R&B singer coming out of the woodwork to sue Vastola. If anyone had, Vastola would not have been as cool as Hesh using the legal system. Vastola was known to go after people in the music business with old-school Mafia methods.

According to Jerry Capeci, the songbird Vastola was never trusted in the mob. He had made millions in loan-sharking and gambling seemingly right under the FBI's nose, yet was never charged with any of these activities. In 1982 he was finally charged with racketeering and won an acquittal in a jury verdict.

John Gotti was convinced that Vastola would someday turn into a rat, and federal agents taped Gotti plotting a hit on him. In 1992, that planned hit brought one of the charges for which Gotti was sent away for life.

While Vastola was lucky in that Gotti never got around to killing him, he wasn't lucky with his last stab at getting into the music industry. In 1985 Vastola went to Philadelphia to strongarm John LaMonte—a record label executive. When LaMonte balked at Vastola's offer to take over his record label and refused to play ball with the mobster, Vastola let go with the punch that made him into a Mafia legend. He punched LaMonte once and knocked him out with a severely broken jaw. Word got out that Vastola was one tough cookie. But not tough enough to beat the assault and extortion charges that were brought against him for punching LaMonte. He was convicted in 1990 and was released from federal prison in 1998. When he was released from jail, he went into retirement and has left the mob life behind.

JUNIOR SOPRANO/JOHN RIGGI

The oldest mob boss on *The Sopranos* is Corrado "Junior" Soprano—played by Dominic Chianese—and he has something of a counterpart in the former boss of the DeCavalcantes, John Riggi. Riggi is now the senior member of the DeCavalcante family, and he wears the big, goofy eyeglasses that "Uncle June" is known for on *The Sopranos*. Both Riggi and Uncle Junior moan about how good the old days were for the mob boys. Riggi was so old-school that he brought back the symbolic gun, knife, and burning holy card Mafia induction ceremony to the DeCavalcante family when they admitted new members. That old tradition had fallen away in New

Jersey, and Riggi wanted New York to know that he would be an old-style Mafia boss.

Junior Soprano and Riggi both kept their mouths shut while on trial for charges from FBI investigations. Uncle Junior had more luck than Riggi in that he got a mistrial on the federal case and wound up at the end of *The Sopranos* in a mental hospital after shooting his nephew, Tony Soprano.

John Riggi was not as lucky. But, like Junior Soprano, he had a good run. Riggi was able to avoid indictment until 1989 when the FBI nailed him on racketeering charges. He was sentenced to twenty years, but like Junior Soprano, he was able to run the family from jail. That is where his luck ran out. In 2003 he faced new charges for murdering a capo in his crew. In 1991 "Fat Louie" LaRossa went to his surprise sixty-fifth birthday party, but never got to blow out the candles on his cake. Riggi had ordered the hit on LaRossa for supposedly making a play to steal Riggi's power.

LaRossa's body was never found, but by 2003 enough members of the DeCavalcante had turned state's evidence that Riggi was indicted on murder charges and will now never see another day as a free man.

TONY SOPRANO/VINNY OCEAN PALERMO

James Gandolfini's character, Tony Soprano, just might be based on Vincent "Vinny Ocean" Palermo. On *The Sopranos*, Tony is a silent partner in a strip club in New Jersey called the Bada Bing. Palermo was also the silent partner of a strip club—his was called Wiggles and was located in New York. Strip clubs are used by the Mafia because they are cash businesses and a lot of profit can be hidden. There is that and, of course, the naked women.

When John Riggi handed over the DeCavalcante reins to the younger Palermo, it was to be a new day for the Jersey mob. Palermo—like Tony Soprano—was responsible for bringing the Mafia into a new millennium. Like Tony Soprano, Vinny Ocean Palermo had to work his way through the mob ranks. Palermo's "Ocean" nickname referred to the fact that he owned a fish store, which was a front for a gambling racket.

Palermo and Tony Soprano are both young men with old-school values, and they mourn the loss of power of the mob. Like his fictional Soprano brother, Palermo was involved in waste management and, even more in character, had a New Jersey private waste management boss killed in 1989, under orders from New York mob boss John Gotti.

Fred Weiss was once the city editor for the *Staten Island Advance* newspaper. That life didn't fulfill him, and he became a bit player in waste management, hooking up with Gotti's crew and some members of the DeCavalcante family. Weiss owned an abandoned railroad yard on Staten Island and had waste removal contracts with some New York hospitals. Weiss was under investigation by the NYPD for dumping infectious wastes near residential neighborhoods.

Gotti feared that if Weiss went to jail he would talk, and he knew far too much about Gotti's Gambino family. Gotti ordered Vinny Palermo to take care of Weiss.

On September 11, 1989 three sedans pulled up to a condo development where Weiss lived with his girlfriend. The condos were on a cul-de-sac, so two of the sedans were used to block access to the building in case Weiss was under NYPD surveillance. Weiss walked out and Palermo shot him four times. He died on the street.

After that hit, things were good for awhile for the DeCavalcantes and Vinny Palermo. The family made money and Palermo lived very large. Things were going well until 1998 when a DeCavalcante member got involved in one of the more harebrained plots in Mafia lore.

In 1998 seven men attacked a Bank of America armored car parked in the basement of the World Trade Center. As the two guards were loading $1.6 million into the truck, the men came at them with guns drawn. They tied up the guards and threw them in the back as they transferred the loot into one of the waiting cars. As the robbery seemed to have been successful, three of the men pulled off the masks they were wearing and smiled—smiled for the cameras trained right on them.

The next day the NYPD released the video, and the police blotter obliged by running the dopey thieves' photos on the front page. By the next day those three were under arrest, and they gave up three others. The only one who had gotten away was DeCavalcante member Ralph Guarino.

Guarino's freedom didn't last long. When he was caught, the FBI kept the arrest hush-hush because they made Guarino a deal he couldn't refuse—turn state's evidence or face a few decades in jail. Guarino signed up to be an informant. His first task was to hand out FBI-bugged cell phones to members of the DeCavalcante family, telling them that he had gotten them free calling minutes for a year. Most members of the DeCavalcante family took Guarino's phones. He was a known operator, and how could they turn down all those free minutes?

Law enforcement officials were amazed that six months later most of the DeCavalcantes were still using the phones. From these phones alone, law enforcement had a mountain of evidence against the family.

Vinny Ocean Palermo was heard on tape saying he no longer trusted Ralph Guarino. Palermo knew Guarino was in on the armed truck robbery in the World Trade Center, and felt that he was a loose cannon and was a danger to the family. With this in mind Palermo met with a few capos in November of 1999 and plotted a hit on Guarino. The feds had heard enough, and on December 2, 1999 Vinny Ocean Palermo and forty other family members were arrested in a huge bust.

By 2000 Palermo saw the evidence against him and joined the Witness Protection Program, becoming the first mob boss ever to do so. His testimony sent scores of his associates away for life.

Palermo—like Tony Soprano—kept a stash of money in a brown paper bag. While Palermo admitted to every crime he or any DeCavalcante member may have committed, the one fact he left out was the $1 million in cash he gave his son, Michael, while in the federal program.

When the feds found out in 2006 about Palermo's dealings, his fate in the program was in jeopardy. His son also faces charges from the IRS for tax evasion. Like the last episode of *The Sopranos*, which aired in June of 2007, we never know what will happen in the end to Tony Soprano or Vinny Palermo.

VIN MAKAZIAN/CORRUPT COPS

John Heard played a local Jersey cop named Vin Makazian on *The Sopranos*. Heard portrayed him as a bloated, broken-down cop with a severe gambling problem. His gambling got so bad that Tony Soprano saw an opportunity, and told the cop that he could work off his debt by doing favors for the Mafia. The cop threw in with the Mafia and threw away his dignity. He did the bidding of criminals, and in the end he could not deal with his conscience and jumped off a bridge on Route 1 in New Jersey.

There have been cases in which cops have joined in with the Mafia. Most incidents never come to light because the crooked cops stop doing their dirty deeds before a case can be made. But some are brazen and make deals with the devil.

In 2005 a New York mobster named Anthony "Gaspipe" Casso went public on *60 Minutes* with Ed Bradley, saying that when he was a mob boss he had plenty of help from the NYPD. Casso claimed that he conspired with "two detectives that work with the major squad team for NYPD."

Casso had been in jail since 1993 for thirty-six admitted murders, and he had told prosecutors that he had corrupt cops on his payroll. At first prosecutors didn't listen because Casso had lied so often. They figured he was looking to cut a deal, and with thirty-six bodies on his resume, he was not a good witness.

But a retired cop, Tommy Dades, who was working as a boxing coach, came out of retirement when he got a solid tip from an informant that Casso wasn't lying about the two corrupt cops. The Brooklyn DA allowed Dades to work in his office and review Casso's allegations. Dades looked up all of the charges against two NYPD detectives, Stephen Caracappa and Louie Eppolito.

One by one they started to come together. Dades couldn't believe what he was finding. Casso had said the cops had run a police computer check on one man and gave Casso his name and address. Casso was looking for a man named Nick Guido, who was trying to put a hit on him. Casso soldiers killed the man on Christmas Day 1986. Dades found that in fact Detective Stephen Caracappa had run a computer check on the man just two weeks before.

The sad thing about the Christmas 1986 hit was that the twenty-six-year-old man who was killed was named Nick Guido—but he was the wrong Nick Guido. The Nick Guido who came up on the police computer was a younger and innocent man who was killed due not only to the Mafia cop's corruption, but also his incompetence.

The wrong Guido was a good man and had no criminal record. He was home for Christmas dinner and took his uncle outside to show off the new car he had gotten as a Christmas present. As he sat in the driver's seat, a man walked up and shot Guido four times in front of his uncle. Nick Guido was dead before he got to the hospital. The killer walked away into the cold night.

Casso told prosecutors that he had learned of Nick Guido when he killed another man in September of 1986—Jimmy Hydell, who was brought to him by the two detectives he had on his payroll.

The two cops had picked up Hydell, who had crossed Casso and had botched a hit on him. "They put him in the car. The kid thought they were taking him to the station house." Casso said. They drove him to a warehouse and pulled him out of the car. They bound and gagged him and threw him into the trunk of a waiting car. The car brought Hydell to Casso, and he took his sweet time killing him. Casso tortured Hydell until he told him that Nick Guido was also involved in the plot. Casso told prosecutors that he had paid the two cops $45,000 for the job of bringing Hydell to him.

Dades was astonished when he found that Hydell's mother identified the two cops, saying they had come to her door looking for her son the day before he was murdered.

For their dirty deeds as cops working with the mob, Caracappa and Eppolito were paid $4,000 a month—each—by Casso. In exchange for that money, Casso was able to check confidential police files on any of his enemies or associates. He was able to use information from police computers to find the location of anyone in New York. Casso knew which clubs and offices were being bugged. For more money, he even got the two cops to kill for him.

In 1990 Casso paid Eppolito and Caracappa $75,000 to kill mobster Eddie Lino. The cops caught up with Lino on a highway and pulled him over. The mobster thought he was getting a speeding ticket. Instead he got three bullets in the head fired by Eppolito and Caracappa.

This was explosive stuff, and cops and prosecutors were very careful in investigating these cops. They took their time, and when the NYPD and Brooklyn prosecutors had enough evidence, they started to slowly drop a net on the two Mafia cops.

One of the cops, Louie Eppolito, had retired from the NYPD in 1990. In 1992 he coauthored *Mafia Cop*, a book about his self-proclaimed exploits as a New York cop and his family's involvement in the Mafia. Eppolito's father was a low-level member of the Mafia, and his uncle was a capo. Throughout the book Eppolito bragged that he was tempted to join the mob life but kept himself clean.

He moved on from the NYPD to act in some minor roles in mob films. He even appeared in the Mafia classic *Goodfellas*. But bigger film roles did not come, so in 1992 Eppolito took his police pension and bought a 4,000-square-foot house in Las Vegas.

His partner, Stephen Caracappa, retired from the NYPD in 1992 and joined Eppolito in Las Vegas. They lived in the same subdivision on the same block, and for two retired cops they were living pretty well.

When the investigation was complete in 2005, the NYPD handed the case to the FBI. Law enforcement officials felt they had a better chance of getting a conviction in federal court than they would in a state court. Caracappa and Eppolito were arrested in Las Vegas. The headlines of police blotters in the New York papers screamed about "Mafia Cops."

In 2006 the pair was found guilty of taking part in eight murders for the Casso crew. Eppolito and Caracappa remain partners, as they will finish out their time doing life sentences sharing a cell in a federal prison.

•••

Even when local cops do go up against the Mafia, they are limited by their lack of jurisdiction and by fellow officers on the take.

While working for the *Kansas City Star*, J. J. Maloney reported on a legendary Kansas City cop named Robert Heinen. Heinen was supposedly a *Dirty Harry*–style cop years before Clint Eastwood took his star turn in that police role. Heinen worked for the Kansas City PD from 1946 until his retirement in 1974 and had a mercurial career.

After he retired, Heinen wrote *The Battle Behind the Badge*, a book in which he alleges that the Kansas City PD was controlled by the local Mafia for years. The book is one-sided, and Heinen explains away his misdeeds as a cop while scolding every other cop. Maloney has a fairer take on Heinen than the cop does in his own book.

Maloney allows that Heinen was hated by the local Mafia because he was one of the few cops in Kansas City who would take them on. Heinen would invade their gambling dens and arrest everyone in the room. He would walk in with a sawed-off pool cue and K-9 dogs as he smacked the mobsters around. Heinen's attacks on the Mafia did not go over well with his Kansas City PD superiors. In 1959 he was demoted from detective to uniformed cop. He plotted to blackmail his bosses to get his rank back. To this end, he broke into the Produce Club, which was frequented by one of Kansas City's biggest mobsters, Carl Civella. He planted an electronic bug that was hooked up to a voice-activated recorder. Heinen claims he caught Civella and a Kansas City PD lieutenant talking about how Civella would have to increase his bribes to the cops up the food chain.

Heinen told his superiors what he had on tape and threatened that if he didn't get what he wanted—his detective job back—he would release the tapes to the prosecutor. Heinen got his job back, but word got out that he had these revealing tapes.

When a grand jury commenced to pursue police corruption, Heinen refused to release the tapes. "Word circulated that I had taped conversations," Heinen recalled, "These tapes were my personal property to be used as a matter of protection and a matter of survival."

Heinen never did release the tapes, and as Maloney writes, "as long as Heinen got what he wanted—detective status and promotions—his corrupt superiors could get away with anything they wanted."

In 1974 Heinen went to war with a new police chief, and it was a losing battle. As he was about to face a departmental hearing, he retired so he could keep his pension. Kansas City locals liked Heinen, and when he turned in his badge, graffiti appeared on numerous walls in the city with the legend, "Viva Heinen."

With his book, Heinen had the last word, and his police career is extolled on the Kansas City PD Web site. He lives on in retirement in Kansas City with his wife, three daughters, and eleven grandchildren. The Mafia in Kansas City is still in full operation.

•••

Local cops have difficulty fighting organized crime because the Mafia wields a lot of local power. For years there have been rumors throughout American cities that there were cops on the Mafia payroll. The famed "Hat Squad" in Los Angeles was a group of tough LA cops who would meet out of town gangsters trying to horn in on the LA crime scene. The cops would beat the mobsters senseless and send them back from whence they came. This kept Los Angeles safe for the mobsters who were there, and many a payoff was made to keep this arrangement going. These cases rarely see the light of day while the cops are on the force.

An example of this is in Chinook, Montana. Now, when someone says the Mafia is operating in Chinook, Montana, everybody laughs or says that there is no truth to it. Everybody except two former police chiefs.

Chinook is in Blaine County in northwest Montana. The city has a population of 1,500 residents, and is the biggest town in the county. In the 1980s the chief of police, Jerry Liese, observed a number of suspicious small planes landing at a modest airstrip in Chinook at 3:00 a.m. The planes were met by a local banker driving a van. He picked up some rough-looking men, and they all headed to the county attorney's home.

Liese had a small force of five officers, but he kept up surveillance of the small planes. Each one was met by the banker, and they always went to the head attorney's home. Liese had various connections in law enforcement and was told that the Mafia was likely using Chinook as a portal for illegal drugs coming into America from Canada. Liese took his findings to the city attorney of Chinook and told him of his suspicions. Liese was told by the attorney, "Leave it alone."

Liese would not leave it alone and kept up his watch. He tried to pursue the matter with the FBI, but he soon found himself under indictment from the county attorney for police brutality. He was relieved of his command, and he stood trial. A jury found him not guilty, and Liese left Chinook for a police job in southern Montana.

Liese told the *Big Sky Gazette* his side of the story, and they published some unflattering columns about the corruption in Blaine County. Bernie Brost, the police chief of Chinook before Liese, was interviewed. When asked if Liese's story was credible, Brost wouldn't comment. When asked why he left his job, all Brost would say was, "You can't fight the Big Boys."

No one was ever indicted in Chinook, but the planes flying in at all hours have stopped. Montana is a big state with plenty of room to land a plane, so it is likely that if there was some nefarious enterprise going on, the spotlight Liese put on Chinook would be enough to make it move elsewhere.

•••

To break the Mafia's hold on a city, the FBI is needed. In 1994 Len Davis was a New Orleans police officer who fell into an unholy agreement with a mob-backed cocaine ring in the Crescent City. He supplied police protection to the warehouse where the cocaine was stashed. His payment was envelopes stuffed with cold, hard cash.

Davis was a dangerous cop and had been investigated many times by Internal Affairs. He was known as a rogue cop, but the New Orleans PD was ineffective at policing its own. An FBI task force was set up, and it observed Davis and ten other cops, in full uniform and driving police cruisers, taking bribes from the coke dealers for their protection.

The FBI set up their own fake mob-backed coke racket and approached Davis, asking him for protection. The FBI warehouse had 286 pounds of cocaine, and nearly $100,000 in bribes was passed to Davis and his cops. For six months the feds clocked the brazen exploits of this crew of renegade cops, and then closed the jailhouse door on all of them. In 1995, all eleven were sentenced to twenty-five-year terms or longer, and all remain guests in the Louisiana prison system.

This corruption of cops by the Mafia is endemic throughout America. In 1998 the General Accounting Office in Washington, DC, conducted a survey citing examples of drug- and mob-related police corruption in Atlanta, Chicago, Cleveland, Detroit, Los Angeles, Miami, New Orleans, New York, Philadelphia, Savannah, and Washington, DC.

CHAPTER 9

stupid is as stupid does

TALK TO ANY COP AND he will tell you the two most valuable police tools in catching a criminal are informants and the criminal's own stupidity. Criminal savvy is overrated. Most felons fall prey to a stupid kind of pride and think everyone is dumber than they are. They are not, and that is why jails are full of criminals still not convinced that their own lack of brainpower is the cause for their incarceration.

Recently in Des Moines, Iowa, a young man walked into a Git-N-Go store and announced a stickup. He had perfected the tough guy look, and cursed and threatened to shoot the clerk with a gun. His only problem was that he had no gun—he was pointing his finger in his coat pocket, and the clerk could see his thumb sticking out. The clerk realized he had a finger pointed at him. He just smiled at the would-be bandit.

"I have a gun!" yelled the bandit.

"No, you don't," countered the clerk. "You have a finger."

"Gun!"

The robber became frustrated and ran outside the store, shaking his head at losing the argument. The clerk called the cops, and the man ran off, looking at his hand like he was wishing it would turn into a gun.

On the Des Moines police Web site, Sergeant David Coy said, "Think about it. When you play cops and robbers, how do you hold your hand? With the thumb sticking up, right?"

Put the emphasis on the word *play*.

•••

On February 2, 2007, Paul Paris, fifty-four, was released from a San Francisco halfway house wearing the same clothes he had been wearing when he went to jail many years before. He was all styled-out in his vintage Members Only jacket on his way to meet his probation officer, whom he did meet, faithfully. And he had another appointment that day: he robbed a bank.

Later that week Paris robbed two more. The SFPD got a good photo of him, and his probation officer saw it. The probation officer didn't recognize Paris's face, but he did recognize that sweet Members Only jacket. Paris was arrested and is now facing some serious jail time. He is also probably the last member of Members Only.

The name Paris connects to stupid criminal behavior on the East Coast, too. In Brooklyn in the mid 1990s, a juvenile delinquent named Paris Little would get arrested once a month by the cops in the 84th Precinct. Since Paris Little was only twelve and quite small, he became something of a law enforcement mascot. None of his crimes were violent, just stupid.

He would bite an apple, put it back on the fruit stand, and then just hang out while the owner called the cops. Or he would steal a shirt from the Gap and then try to return it. Given his age, the cops would take him to Family Court where he would sit. No parent ever showed up for Paris. The court officers called him "Little Paris Little."

One spring day as he was waiting to appear before a judge, Paris wrote "Paris Little Was Here" on the courtroom door. An officer who saw it shook his head and realized that there was no hope. Paris Little certainly was there, was going to be there, and would eventually stay there. The judge, tired of Paris's extensive record, sent him to a juvenile facility for one year, and again no parent bothered to show up at the sentencing.

•••

Statistics show that victims are better off fighting a mugger, rather than succumbing to his demands. Running away is also a good, solid choice. Cops probably prefer that you not know that, but it is true, and given how stupid some criminals are, we all stand a fighting chance.

The AP reported on February 22, 2007, that three bandits boarded a tour bus full of American senior citizens outside of Limón, Costa Rica. One bandit was Warner Segura, twenty, and with him were two unnamed accomplices. They demanded the seniors empty their pockets.

One seventy-year-old, crusty army veteran would have none of this nonsense. He jumped up, grabbed the much younger Segura in a headlock, and snapped his clavicle. The other seniors became emboldened and fought off the other two bandits, who were armed with a knife and a gun. They ran away, leaving the injured Segura behind.

The tour bus took Segura to a hospital, where he died from his injury. The army vet had killed the man. Limón chief of police Luis Hernandez said no charges would be filed against the American, explaining that "the seniors were in their rights to defend themselves after being held up."

•••

Ricky Pickett from Brooklyn was a stupid but dangerous criminal. In April of 1990 when New York was going through its last real crime wave of the twentieth century, men like Ricky Pickett were legion. Most did not meet the same fate as Pickett, but the old saying about a life of crime having only three outcomes—jail, a mental institution, or death—is true.

On Thursday, April 12, 1990, Ricky Pickett was hanging out in the Van Dyke Projects in Brooklyn. Pickett was bad news, a three-time convicted felon and a serial mugger always on the lookout for a victim. Pickett thought he was invulnerable and that no one was badder than he was. That would prove to be a fatal conceit.

On that cool April night Pickett was with four friends. They broke out some cheap wine, smoked blunts, and talked about how they were going to get some money. Statistics show that in America the most dangerous day for crime is the Thursday before Christmas. In fact, Thursdays throughout the year are dangerous because by that day of the week, the criminals know they don't have enough money for any kind of fun on the weekend.

On this particular Thursday, Pickett and his crew needed some coin. The neighborhood in Brooklyn where Pickett lived was dirt-poor and tough, so he and his crew boarded a 4 train and headed into Manhattan, following an old Brooklyn thug motto: "Manhattan makes it and Brooklyn takes it."

To a thug like Pickett, Manhattan was full of soft, rich folks who would gladly hand over their money. With mugging in mind, Pickett and his crew moved from subway car to subway car looking for a victim to pay for their night out in the city. Pickett found a middle-aged white man sitting by himself and told his posse, "I'm going shopping. This one is real."

It was 10:45 p.m. when Ricky Pickett slowly approached the man. With a violent fury he picked the man up and threw him down on the floor. The man covered his midsection as the crew pounded him, and then went through his pockets and grabbed his wallet. Pickett lifted the man up and threw him into the seat, wanting to have some fun.

This is why Ricky Pickett was stupid—not just in the usual sense of "stupid," but also in the street sense. Instead of taking the wallet and running, he wanted a pound of flesh. But suddenly the victim wasn't cowering anymore. He kicked two of the thugs away, and then pulled out a silver-plated .38 and shot Pickett three times in the chest.

Two of the goons ran off the train as it pulled into the Court Street station in Brooklyn. Two others ducked into another car, hoping the shooter wouldn't follow them. The man calmly picked up his hat, which the thugs had knocked off his head, and left the train, disappearing into the Brooklyn night.

Ricky Pickett remained. He was able to get up and followed his friends into the other car. They looked at him with horror as blood rushed from a gaping hole in his chest. He tried to say something, but crashed to the floor. Before the train doors closed, his two friends ran off. The train pulled out of the last station in Brooklyn. By the time it reached Manhattan, Pickett was dead. Instead of spending the night clubbing in Manhattan, he died alone on the floor of a subway car.

News of the incident hit the police blotter the next morning, and New Yorkers, blacks and whites alike, seemed pleased that a mugger like Ricky Pickett had met his end in such a fitting manner. The NYPD made a cursory effort to catch the shooter. The cops interviewed Pickett's crew and got a laugh when the thieves claimed that the man was mugging them. The muggers finally came clean and sold out Pickett, putting the onus of the crime on him. Within a week the lead detective on the case said they had no luck and the case was essentially closed. No one was hot to solve Ricky Pickett's murder.

Peg Tyre, who covered the Pickett shooting for *Newsday*, said, "With that shooting, people started to think that maybe it wouldn't be so bad if some vigilantism came creeping in. There was a sense throughout the city that Ricky Pickett got what he deserved. No one was weeping over his death."

But the big question remained: Who shot wicked Ricky Pickett? No one was ever arrested, but the scuttlebutt in the law enforcement community was that the mugger picked the wrong man to mug—the "victim" might have been a cop, court officer, corrections officer, or other lawman who shot a man off duty and decided not to turn himself in. Maybe he chose to cut and run rather than face a Brooklyn jury.

The reason for thinking that the man was in law enforcement was the way he wisely took the beating and kept his gun safe. Pickett assumed the man was not armed. The shooter had the presence of mind to go for his gun at just the right moment. He shot three bullets into Pickett's chest, just like cops train to do at the firing range.

Then there is the matter of the wallet. Pickett's friends did steal the man's wallet and the police recovered it, but the cops said the wallet was not the shooter's. They never did say whose wallet it was, and no one ever bothered to ask.

•••

In contrast to the angry stupidity of someone like Ricky Pickett, Claude King was just weird, silly stupid.

In February 2007, King, thirty-one, stole a GMC Envoy in Boca Raton, Florida. King was not much of a driver and wound up crashing the vehicle twice. He drove away after each fender bender and eventually realized he was lost.

Here's the clincher: You know how men don't like to ask for directions because they don't want to admit they're lost? (Yeah, it's a macho thing.) Well, King didn't want to ask anyone for directions, so he just decided *to give himself up*.

The AP reported that King called the Palm Beach police and said, "Um, I committed a crime. I stole a vehicle. I've been a bad boy. I believe a spanking is in order."

Spanking?

The dispatcher asked King where he was. King said he was lost, so how would he know? It took awhile for the cops to find King, but they finally grabbed him as he sat on the curb by the stolen SUV in Palm Beach. He was charged with grand theft auto, but police would not comment on whether he ever got that spanking.

•••

Speaking of spanking, a seven-year-old girl from Burnett, Wisconsin, could use one. Children that young aren't named on police blotter stories, but even kids can do some stupid things that make cops shake their heads.

The little girl was home with her grandfather, and to pass the time they decided to play a game of cards. The girl was very competitive and got angry when her Grandpa won a few hands. She left the card table steamed, grabbed the phone, and dialed 911. As soon as a dispatcher picked up, the little girl panicked and hung up the phone.

Most towns send a patrol cop when 911 makes contact with a home phone, regardless of what is said. The dispatcher sent an RMP, otherwise known as a cop car, to check out the call. When the cops knocked on the door, the little girl ran to them and said she wanted to report her grandfather for cheating while playing cards. The grandfather explained that the girl had just learned about using 911 and guessed she had overestimated the list of legal complaints. The cops just let it go. But the moral of that story is that even your grandchild can rat you out.

•••

Of course, adults also call 911 when they shouldn't. *New York Post* wire services reported in November of 2006 that a Wichita, Kansas, man dialed to report that he had been robbed. Not just any robbery, but a home invasion by a man waving a sawed-off shotgun. When the cops got to the house they asked the man what was taken.

The man hesitated and then admitted that the thief had stolen more than a pound of marijuana. The cops called in for a drug-sniffing dog to see if the thief had missed anything. He had. The dog found some more pot, and the "victim" was arrested. The thief who got away with the pound of pot is still at large, and possibly very stoned.

•••

The police blotter hit bottom when Christopher Willever, twenty-two, stood in an Omaha, Nebraska, courtroom, contrite as he awaited his sentence. Judge Thomas Otepka gave him three to five years for robbing a store called the Tobacco Hut in Omaha. Otepka added, "You were an ass in every true sense of the word in this crime."

What raised Otepka's ire was the publicity that Willever's crime received. As his attorney explained in court, Willever was tired of being poor. With that in mind he went out and drank a quart of rum and decided to break into the Tobacco Hut. That he did, but what he didn't expect was his pants falling down. He also didn't take into account that the store had security cameras that filmed his bare behind as he ransacked the store like a drunken bear. Video from the store's cameras showed up on nearly every midwest TV station, and on the Internet site YouTube.com. The slightly hazy video depicts Willever as a fat bumbling dope with a fat ass and a bad sense of balance. It was not a pretty performance.

Willever became known as the Bare Bottom Burglar and is now in prison, where one can only hope that Willever keeps his pants up.

•••

Robert Marsh, thirty-nine, was no stranger to the criminal justice system. He had served some very long years as the chained guest of the Wisconsin prison system, and it seemed he couldn't stay out of jail.

In 2006 in Fond Du Lac, Wisconsin, Marsh broke through a deadbolt on a house door and grabbed the woman who lived there. It was 3:00 a.m., and she let out a scream that awoke two men who also lived in the house. They seized Marsh and called 911. When the Fond Du Lac Sheriff's Department arrested Marsh, he told them he was a shape-changing werewolf, which allowed him access to the house.

Getting busted for criminal trespassing and possession of marijuana might explain Marsh's lupine hallucinations, but that didn't get him any pardons. He was sent back to jail, where he might still be working on his shape changing.

•••

In February 2007, the LAPD went into action in front of Grauman's Chinese Theatre to arrest a six-foot-five, forty-four-year-old man dressed as Chewbacca—the Wookiee from *Star Wars*—for harassing Japanese tourists and head-butting a Hollywood tour guide who tried to make the big fellow stop bothering his clients.

In the police complaint the Wookiee was quoted as saying, "Nobody tells this Wookiee what to do," before smacking his head into the tour guide's noggin. A bystander dressed as Superman was a witness to the attack.

Grauman's Chinese Theatre is no stranger to weird characters in costumes making the police blotter. In 2005, enthusiasts dressed like Mr. Incredible, Elmo, and the Hulk were arrested for aggressive panhandling outside the theater. (The police blotter didn't report whether tourists found Elmo or the Hulk more sympathetic.)

LAPD charged the Wookiee with misdemeanor battery, and the alien was released on $20,000 bail. This was the first case of a resident of the planet Endor being taking into LAPD custody, although there have been cases of Ewoks getting off with just a warning.

Hey, it's LA.

•••

Sometimes those dressed in costumes can save the day. And sometimes grown men can be scared off by children.

In 2006 in Durham, North Carolina, two thugs barged into Jennifer Long's apartment armed with a gun. The thugs made her empty her purse and grabbed all the money, ATM cards, and jewelry that had spilled out. One of the felons pointed the gun at her five-year-old daughter Mary and threatened to shoot her if the mother did not comply.

With the ATM cards in hand, one man left to bring the getaway car around to the front of the house. The other man held his gun on the child and Long, and told her they would be taking her to a bank to empty her account. Jennifer Long had a secret weapon that the thieves did not know about. Her four-year-old son, Stevie, had snuck away to his bedroom and was putting on his Mighty Morphin Power Ranger Halloween costume.

Little Stevie Long burst into the living room in his red outfit with his plastic sword at the ready and swooped down on the burglars, swinging his blade and yelling, "Yah! Yah! Get away from my family."

The cop who took the call for the Durham PD said, "During the robbery a . . . boy snuck into the bedroom, dressed himself in a Power Ranger costume, and armed himself with a plastic sword. The child exited the room and approached the armed suspect, in an attempt to protect his family."

A relative of Stevie's claimed that the robber gave up the idea of taking Long to the ATM to withdraw cash after the display of Power Ranger courage. "It totally tripped the robber out, and that's when they moved on," the relative said.

A four-year-old armed with a plastic sword was able to scare off a grown man with a gun—a rare feat. Most police will tell you that the Might Morphin Power Rangers, while courageous in their hearts, are no match for an actual firearm, so don't get any ideas about pulling on the costume when there's trouble.

•••

Movie actor Paul Sorvino is a sworn deputy in Monroe County, Pennsylvania. How he went from starring in *Goodfellas* to being a volunteer lawman is anyone's guess. Along with a badge, Sorvino is allowed to carry a gun, and due to the 2002 Patriot Act, any active lawman sanctioned to carry a gun can carry one in any state in America.

On January 3, 2007 this came in handy for Sorvino, although when the papers got word of his "police action," Monroe County may have regretted making him a deputy. Sorvino's daughter, thirty-six-year-old Amanda, was in Stowe, Vermont, when she dumped her ne'er-do-well twenty-one-year-old boyfriend, Daniel Snee. Snee was heartbroken, so he got liquored up (standard operating procedure for a lot of guys), went to the motel where Amanda Sorvino was staying, and went wild.

In fear, Amanda called 911, and also called her father who was at another nearby hotel. Pistol-packing Papa Sorvino arrived faster than the cops.

Officer Fredrick Whitcomb of the Stowe police wrote in his report, "He [Sorvino] told Snee to leave the motel, but Snee would not and was acting aggressive. Sorvino told me that he pulled out his gun and was preparing to fire a warning shot because he thought Snee was going to attack him, but the police arrived."

A warning shot? See—that is the trouble with deputizing a movie star. There is no such thing as a warning shot. All police are trained never to pull their weapon unless their intent is to use it, and never to fire unless it is necessary. Warning shots lost favor in the 1930s after numerous people were hit by stray bullets. Maybe Sorvino was watching too many old B movies, but he clearly shouldn't be carrying a gun and a badge. Acting isn't training for real life.

Snee was no rocket scientist either. He had a blood alcohol level of .178—twice the legal limit in Vermont—and was put into a cruiser to be arrested on charges of domestic violence and disorderly conduct. The arresting officer walked away to take a statement from Paul and Amanda Sorvino, and Snee managed to open the car door and flee into the cold woods. He was found a minute later hiding behind a tree.

Paul Sorvino had no comment about any of this. Amanda went home to Pennsylvania and filed a restraining order against Snee. Papa Sorvino might want to put a restraining order on himself before he shoots someone.

•••

On January 31, 2007, two young men in Boston put up electric light boxes around the city. The boxes were part of the Cartoon Network's guerilla-marketing ad campaign for a show called *Aqua Teen Hunger Force*. The boxes flashed the date 1/31/07; the image of a character in the show, Moon Man, giving the finger; and the words NEVER FORGET on the bottom. The boxes, posted on buildings and abutments, had visible wires and batteries. With a little imagination, and perhaps a little paranoia, they could have passed for bombs, and that they did: the Boston 911 system was flooded with calls, and the city police responded in force, calling out its SWAT and anti-terror teams, effectively shutting Boston down for hours. For a brief time, many in law enforcement thought the situation was the real thing—improvised explosive devices (IEDs) sprinkled all over Boston.

While most memories of 9/11 focus on New York City, Washington, DC, and Pennsylvania, Bostonians are well aware of their city's connection to that day of infamy. Boston Police Commissioner Thomas Menino, quoted in various newspapers, said, "Just a little over a mile away from the placement of the first [*Aqua Teen*] device, a group of terrorists boarded airplanes and launched an attack on New York City"—a statement that neatly folded together the perverted nature of our modern world in which cartoon-network gimmicks can very easily and quickly conjure the memory of actual horrors.

Peter Berdovsky, twenty-seven, and Sean Stevens, twenty-eight, two men employed by the Cartoon Network, were arrested for the light-box stunt, and were charged with placing a hoax device (an actual charge in the Boston police code) and disorderly conduct. They were released on bail, and when the press met them shortly after their release, the young men spoke only about their hair (Berdovsky wore immense dreadlocks).

"For example, Afros, I think, come kind of from the seventies, but then again there's other styles," Berdovsky said as he shook his long, matted 'do.

Stevens added, "Hair today, gone tomorrow."

Remember, these guys worked for the Cartoon Network, not al Qaeda.

Turner Broadcasting, the parent company of the Cartoon Network, agreed to pay Boston $2 million for the police cost to the city. On March 7, Berdovsky and Stevens appeared in court but had no further quips for the media. A hoax charge is a felony, so the two hirsute fellows were nice and quiet before the judge. At the time of this writing, the DA and the defense lawyers were reported to be working out a settlement for the two clowns that would allow them not to do jail time.

Here's the kicker: Persons unknown took hold of some of the offending light boxes and auctioned them on eBay. On the same day that Berdovsky and Stevens were in court, bids for the contraband light boxes rose as high as $347. Someday you might see one hanging in some décor-obsessed person's living room, and you'll be staring at a wild tale from the police blotter.

•••

Being a police officer does not protect you from stupidity if you decide to cross the line and get into crime. Cops who go bad are some of the stupidest criminals out there. Maybe it is because to go that route, something has to be wrong with the hardwiring in the brain. Every police officer knows the most dangerous place on earth for a cop is prison, and this fact alone keeps most in line. But not all.

On a cold winter night in January 2007, Jeanne Kane sat in her car outside a Staten Island train station waiting to pick up her daughter. Kane was listening to a soft rock station. At fifty-eight, she still had the musical chops of her youth. She was once a member of the group the Kane Sisters, a triplet singing act that performed on Ed Sullivan and Perry Como's TV shows in the 1960s. She and her sisters never made the big time, and in 1976 Kane settled down in a New Jersey suburb and married a New York cop, John Galtieri. They had one child.

In 1980 Galtieri had retired from the NYPD and got a nice three-quarter disability pension. He put out a shingle and began working as a private investigator. He started to make some serious money. He should have been happy. He wasn't. In his spare time he took to beating his wife.

Kane endured as long as she could, but the marriage ended in 2003. A judge found that Jeanne Kane was a battered woman and awarded her $400,000 plus a percentage of Galtieri's pension. Galtieri also had to give her half the proceeds from the sale of their New Jersey home, $30,000 in jewelry, and $2,200 a month in alimony for life.

Galtieri took the hit, moved to Punta Gorda, Florida, and remarried. He kept up his PI work, but became a bitter man. His new wife also had him arrested for hitting her, but then dropped the charges. Galtieri was filled with strange demons and a mighty foul temper. He could not let go of his anger toward his first wife. He felt the court had screwed him in the divorce settlement, and he decided to do something about it.

He drove up to New York, and on Friday, January 26, 2007, he filed an order to show cause to stop Kane from getting a piece of his pension and any alimony due. He showed up in court in a rage and stalked out of the courthouse when the case was adjourned. That weekend he got the brilliant idea that instead of paying his ex-wife, he could kill her and be free and clear of her forever.

The following Monday, Galtieri followed Kane to the parking lot of the train station, and as she listened to the radio, he shot her once in the face through the passenger-side window. Of course, Galtieri should have known better. The first person the cops look for when a woman is killed is her husband or ex-husband. Galtieri had no alibi, and everyone knew he was in New York for the court appearance.

After killing Kane, Galtieri ran to his car. He picked a stupid spot for his crime. The train station where he killed his ex-wife was under surveillance by scores of security cameras. He should have known that most train stations in New York have these cameras. Since 9/11 New York City has become the most filmed city in history, except for contemporary London, and possibly Las Vegas. Security cameras are everywhere, and the cops got a good look at John Galtieri hightailing into his car.

The NYPD put out an allpoints bulletin for Galtieri, and the next day South Carolina cops nabbed him as he was trying to return to his Florida home. The South Carolina trooper who arrested him claimed that Galtieri was a perfect gentleman and didn't seem the type who would kill a defenseless woman. His former police partners disagreed and, while not giving their names, labeled the former cop "an angry nut job."

Galtieri lawyered up and had his attorney, Harris Beach, claim that Galtieri "denies doing it or ever being anywhere in the vicinity" of the killing of Jeanne Kane.

Beach must not have known about the security camera that showed his client fleeing the scene. When the NYPD went to South Carolina to take Galtieri back to New York to face second-degree murder charges, Beach filed a motion that Galtieri could not fly because he suffered panic attacks when he flew.

The papers in New York had a field day with that. They compared it the plot from the 1988 Robert DeNiro movie, *Midnight Run*. In that flick, DeNiro plays a bounty hunter whose prisoner, Charles Grodin, claims he can't fly due to panic attacks. DeNiro takes Grodin on a wild odyssey in cars and trains.

In the reports from his interrogation in South Carolina, Galtieri moaned to the cops, "I don't have any income—my wife gets it all. Can you believe I only get seven dollars out of my retirement. . . . I live paycheck to paycheck."

Galtieri told the cops he had been in New York City to try to keep more of his monthly $2,777 NYPD pension. He denied killing Jeanne Kane and said he was in the lot because he was getting some sleep before driving home to Florida.

But perhaps the depth and width of his stupidity finally sank in, because Galtieri waived an extradition trial and was put on a train back to New York City shackled and in the custody of two NYPD detectives. He had no comment as he got off the train to face the music back in New York. There's no explaining fleeing a murder scene on camera.

•••

In Tempe, Arizona, another cop joined in the Stupid Hall of Fame when he decided to take hip-hop out of his radio and onto his beat. An episode of a local cable live cop show sanctioned by the Tempe PD, *Tempe Street Beat*, showed Sergeant Chuck Schoville (a white cop) stopping two black men in a car for littering. Schoville made the men an offer: They could beat the $500 ticket he was about to give them if they rapped for him.

One man couldn't resist the deal and spun a rap—"Yo, I just got pulled over 'cause I threw my trash out the window when they rolled over. They got behind me and pulled me over."

Schoville laughed and rapped back, "Because I got a gun and badge, I'm always right. That's the way it works, right?" (Great rhyme, eh?)

After twenty-five years as a cop, the good sergeant should have known better than this. When the show aired, local African-American groups howled discrimination and stereotyping, and the city and the cops shelved the show. Schoville had to issue a public apology, but was not disciplined by the Tempe PD. His audition for *American Idol*, however, is on hold.

•••

Sometimes just pure dumb greed brings down a stupid criminal. Tekle Zigetta worked for years perfecting the art of counterfeiting money. He got his start in his homeland of Korea and then kept it up after becoming a United States citizen.

In January of 2006 Zigetta was busted at the Los Angeles airport for smuggling $37,000 into the country after a visit to Korea. That money was real, but U.S. Customs agents had a hunch he was into funny money.

Customs searched Zigetta's Los Angeles apartment. Sharp-eyed agents found a cache of counterfeit money and put him under arrest. Zigetta was amazed at how quickly he was caught. He asked the customs agents how they knew his money was fake. Was the coloring not right? Was the paper not good to the touch?

The agents assured the artist that he had the colors and the feel for the money right, but they pointed to the $250 billion in *billion-dollar* bills that they had found. Zigetta apparently did not realize that there is no such currency in America as a billion-dollar bill. These fake American billion-dollar bills featured Grover Cleveland's portrait and a stamp of the year 1934. Had Zigetta studied his civics book, he would have learned that the biggest bill in America is the $100,000 bill, featuring Woodrow Wilson's mug. That bill is used exclusively between government agencies; not a single note is in circulation.

Zigetta faced fifteen years in jail, plenty of time to study American monetary history.

•••

Perhaps it's not always greed that makes a crook a mental dullard, but rather another of the seven deadly sins: pride. In 2006 the AP reported that a sixteen-year mystery was solved when a man pled guilty to stealing a double-action six-shot .38-caliber Colt revolver used by President Theodore Roosevelt in the famous battle of San Juan Hill, in the 1898 Spanish-American War.

In April of 1990, Anthony Tulino took a tour of Roosevelt's home at the Sagamore Hill National Historical Site in Oyster Bay, Long Island. The gat was in a case that had no alarm, and Tulino, who was alone, grabbed it, stuck it under his shirt, and left the home.

Tulino later left New York and moved to Deland, Florida, and took up work as a mailman. When people visited his home, he couldn't help showing off his prize gun. People marveled at the gun's inscription: "July 1st, 1898, San Juan, Carried and Used by Colonel Theodore Roosevelt, From the Sunken Battleship *Maine*."

The gun was valued at $500,000 and had been recovered from the wreck of the *Maine* by one of Teddy's many relations. It had been given to the Rough Rider by his fellow soldiers so he could remember the *Maine* by shooting Spaniards.

The FBI received a tip from one of the people Tulino had allowed to see his prized possession. An unknown person apparently knew his guns and his history, and had respect for both. The feds arrested Tulino, and he later pled guilty to a violation of the American Antiquities Act of 1906, which had been signed into law by Roosevelt himself. It looked like Teddy reached out from the grave to help collar Tulino. The gun-snatcher received ninety days in jail and a $500 fine. The gun went to its new, alarm-rigged case.

•••

Timothy Tietjen, thirty-two, from Long Island, New York, came up with a way to beat the heavy traffic on the Long Island Expressway. He had a dummy used for practicing CPR, which he taped to a box and put in the front seat of his car. When he drove to and from work ,he could jump into the high-occupancy vehicle (HOV) lanes, which required two or more people in a car.

The HOV lanes are speedy, and Tietjen was very pleased with his scam. He was saving twenty minutes on his commute. He got away with it for months until a Suffolk County trooper, Thomas Daly, saw the two dummies in the car. Daly told the *New York Post*, "This person either looks dead or is not real. It did not appear lifelike."

Daly pulled over Tietjen and saw the CPR dummy. The trooper said the driver had a "cat that ate the canary look." Daly wrote Tietjen a $90 summons and alerted his commander to the ruse. Daly had heard tales that this kind of dummy con was going on but he had never witnessed it before.

Tietjen found the whole thing funny, and declared that for all the months he had gotten away with his dummy ploy, the $90 was well worth it. He also said that he was keeping the dummy, and who knows? He may take him out again for another ride.

•••

If you are going to hire a hit man, you have to make sure the guy you hire really is a legit assassin. If not, there could be trouble. The guy could botch the job, turn the tables on you and whack you instead of your target, or wear a wire and send your butt to stir. And if you're going to hire someone to kill a police commissioner, you might want to make sure the killer is not an undercover cop.

David Brown Jr., forty-seven, was sitting in a cell on Rikers Island when he became enraged with New York Police Commissioner Ray Kelly. Brown had been in prison before. He had done a mere six years for the attempted murder of his wife and was back in the hoosegow for violating his parole.

Brown was angry about the death of Sean Bell. Bell and three friends had been shot at fifty-one times by New York cops on his wedding day. Bell was the only man to die. The Bell case went down in November of 2006 and remained a hot police blotter item well into 2007. Brown decided he wanted his own justice, so he offered $15,000 to a man he did not know to chop off Ray Kelly's head.

In newspaper stories, Brown reportedly said, "I want his head chopped off. . . . I want them to feel like I am a . . . terrorist. . . . I want people to feel my wrath and rage."

In a neat little jailhouse setup, Brown had unknowingly reached an undercover NYPD cop by phone when he made his insane offer. To sweeten the deal, Brown also offered the officer another $150,000 to plant a bomb at police headquarters. They had two face-to-face meetings at the prison to iron out the details. When the deal was sealed, Brown was arrested and charged with second-degree criminal solicitation. Brown can add that to the thirty other charges that he has earned throughout his lengthy criminal career.

And Ray Kelly? Long before he was New York City police commissioner, he served a tour in Vietnam with the Marines. Now he's routinely threatened by whack-job criminals in and out of jail. But the guy's never lost his head.

•••

The last thing a kid needs at any youth sporting event is an overbearing parent. And yet, such grownups provide endless entertainment, albeit at the cost of their children's respect.

In September 2006 Cory Petero, thirty-six, from Riverbank, California, proved that point. Petero was the assistant coach of the Riverside Redskins, a Pop Warner football team for thirteen-year-olds. His team was up 16 to 6 in the waning minutes of the opening game when Brian Woods, thirteen, of the opposing team, the Stockton Bears, put a late hit on Petero's son. Dear ol' dad would have none of that, so when the game was winding down, he ran out onto the field and tackled Brian Woods to avenge his son.

Woods went flying and the field broke out into a donnybrook. Parents and kids went at it. Multiple parent-operated camcorders caught the action, and Petero surrendered himself to police. The initial charge was felony child abuse, carrying a sentence of six years of prison. Petero pled down to a misdemeanor and insisted on going to trial. If Petero loses, he could face a year in jail. Woods went on the record that he thinks Petero should do jail time. There was no word on just how ashamed Petero's son was.

•••

Brian Brain (his real name) mugged a man in Brooklyn in August of 2006. Brain's choice of weapon was a brick. He slugged his forty-two-year-old victim over the head on Franklin Avenue in Crown Heights, Brooklyn. All Brain got from the theft was a watch, and he used his twenty-two-year-old legs to run away.

Brain did not used his brain, as he only ran three blocks away and then decided to stop and hang out on the corner. The victim passed by in a cop car and pointed at Brian Brain, and stupid Brain was easily arrested and charged with robbery and assault.

•••

Michael Hunter, thirty-seven, from Kentucky, was traveling through West Virginia when he pulled his car over because he had to urinate. He chose a parking lot as the place to relieve himself, failing to notice that it was the lot for the West Virginia police headquarters in South Charleston.

Hunter relieved himself. Then Trooper J. S. Crane arrested him, post-pee. Crane searched Hunter's vehicle and found a marijuana pipe to add to the public urination charges. How do you explain that to mom?

•••

Breaking *into* a prison is about as stupid as a crime could be, but somehow John Davis, twenty, from Brewton, Alabama, found something even stupider.

Davis scaled the fence of the Escambia, Alabama, county jail to deliver drugs to his best customers: some of the inmates. A security camera caught a bag being lowered from a prison window and Brown taking money from the bag and putting drugs in. He was arrested for promoting prison contraband, drug possession, and criminal trespassing.

Davis was held in the jail he broke into because he could not make the $15,000 bond. Probably no one shared their dope with him.

•••

In September of 2006, Jon Tripp was facing a criminal trial in Marin, California for stealing computers from a local retail merchant. Marin County police claimed that Tripp hid in a bathroom after the courthouse was closed and then used a recycling bin to steal six more computers from the courthouse.

A sharp-eyed sheriff discovered Tripp's plan, foiled it, and arrested him. Tripp then faced a second trial for computer theft in the Marin County Courthouse. Officials promised that Tripp would not have access to any part of the court after it was closed. The computers he tried to steal would later be used in the county's case against him.

•••

The final word goes to a cop who worked on various criminal gang cases for many years. He is still on the job and still undercover, but he said this: "On tape after tape I would hear these criminals laugh at how lame and stupid cops are. How we were a bunch of donut-eating losers. They boasted of their so-called high life and made fun of our middle-class existence.

"But I followed these fools for years, and their lives were terrible. They worked from dawn to dusk trying to make a buck. They could never relax because if the police didn't come to arrest them, their own so-called friends might kill them. I would go home to a warm bed and a nice family when I was done, while they were still out there chasing the illegal buck. Their lives were a mess. Most are now dead or in prison. I have a good life, pride, and a nice pension coming soon. So you tell me: who was stupid?"

epilogue

ONE THING I HAVE LEARNED as a crime reporter is that during any time of economic uncertainty there are four commodities that America—and the world—will never run out of: the wild, the weird, the stupid, and the criminal.

Now, in a book covering wild tales from the police blotter, the problem is not in what to write about but in how to choose just what is wild enough to make the cut. I played enough sports to make it to the final cut, and the times my name was left off on the last cut, it was heart wrenching. I feel the same way for some of the tales I had to drop.

I left so much on the cutting room floor it is almost a shame. Like the story of a man in New York who attacked his cousin over some insipid family dispute and was arrested by the NYPD. When the cops asked him his name, he replied, "How Lame." The cops were convinced he was goofing on them until the man produced a valid ID. How Lame, indeed.

I included some weird sports criminals but left out O. J. Simpson. He was just too easy. After his 2007 Las Vegas arrest for armed robbery, it looked like The Juice was finally going to face the big squeeze. Athletes like O. J., Mike Tyson, and Atlanta Falcons quarterback and dog killer Michael Vick aren't included either. That just felt too much like shooting fish in a barrel. They all had a sign on their asses that read "Kick Me!" and I just couldn't do it. I'll kick you, but when you're down, I can't do it. I'll let the self-righteous pundits handle that crew.

Trevor Berbick was one athlete I wished I could have gotten to. Berbick was a heavyweight boxer who once defeated Muhammad Ali in 1981. That year he also lost a bout to Larry Holmes—Ali's successor to the throne. Berbick had the temerity to take on a twenty-year-old Mike Tyson in 1986. Berbick was the Kevin Bacon of the boxing world, as he was the sole link to Tyson, Holmes, and Ali.

By 1986, Trevor Berbick's best boxing days were behind him, and Mike Tyson beat him like he'd stolen something. But any man willing to get in a ring with Mike Tyson in his heyday has my respect. I met Mike Tyson once in a courtroom hallway. He was polite and shook my hand, but I knew if the mood suited him he'd be able to rip my arms out of their sockets. He was like a feral man who was trying to get along with the weak.

After Tyson beat Berbick like a steel drum, Berbick wound up as a weird tale on the Jamaican police blotter in October of 2006, when he was found hacked to death by some hoods who had a beef with Berbick over a bit of Jamaican land. Maybe they were repaying the former boxer with some karma for beating a washed-up Ali, but this beating was with machetes instead of Everlast boxing gloves. Berbick was dead at fifty-two from four hacks to the head.

Another wild tale concerning sports that didn't make it was from 2006, when the second-string punter for the University of Northern Colorado got an idea on how he could advance his college football career. Mitch Cozad stabbed the school's starting punter in his kicking leg. Cozad jumped Rafael Mendoza in the university's parking lot and stuck a knife right into the thigh of his kicking leg. The police were called and Cozad was arrested.

Cozad's scheme worked—but not in the way he'd planned. While he sat in jail and Mendoza was mending on the bench, the college had to enlist the third-string punter to handle the job.

Then there is the poor working snook who gets on the blotter just because he was trying to do his job. William Connell got lost driving his tractor trailer in a Philadelphia suburb. The cops pulled him to be just to pull someone over and write a speeding ticket; a cop never knows who or what he's going to encounter. And then, on top of that, the cop becomes the officious jerk who won't cut you a break.

It's also easy to read in a newspaper about a cop who shoots someone and then think "Did he really have to kill the guy?" Here is the unspoken code of a cop drawing his weapon: you don't take out your weapon unless you're going to shoot it, and when you shoot, you aim at the chest area, which usually is a fatal shot.

Unless you have had a gun drawn on you by a criminal or have been shot at, you will never know the terror that many cops have to deal with. A cop's description of the job is often as follows: "95 percent boredom and 5 percent terror." It's a hard job that doesn't pay a lot, and most of the men and women in law enforcement truly and honorably protect and serve their communities.

What I wanted to give you in this book is a taste of everything involved in police work—from the weird, strange, and horrible to the funny. Cops are not just cops; at times they also have to be psychologists, referees, medics, pains in the ass (as they write parking tickets), animal trainers, wrestlers, spies, a friendly ear for lonely or hurt people, sharpshooters, and saviors. That's a lot to ask for in one job, but it is this kind of variety in the work that draws people to it.

The last weird tale I have is about a New York cop named Gary Gorman who worked in the Emergency Service Unit. Gorman's specialty was dealing with jumpers.

In 1983 a man climbed up on the Brooklyn Bridge and was yelling to the cops below that he was going to jump. Gorman went up to try and talk him out of it. Gorman told the guy that life was worth living, but the only reply the man had for him was that he liked Gorman's police hat. He asked Gorman if he could hold it. Gorman handed over the hat; the man looked at it and then flung it down into the East River.

Now the guy on the bridge was wearing a baseball hat, so Gorman grabbed that and threw it into the East River. The two stared at each other in anger for moment, and then both men started to laugh. Gorman saw the opening and grabbed the guy, secured him with a rope, and got him safely down from the bridge.

As he recounted the story to his fellow officers, Gorman said, "You know, I'm glad I saved that guy, but I'm still pissed off about my hat."

about the author

This is C. J. Sullivan's second book with The Lyons Press. *1001 Greatest Things Ever Said About New York*, published in 2006, is Sullivan's take on his hometown through some of the funniest, most poignant, and truest things ever said about New York. It's an eclectic collection that features everyone, from Edgar Allen Poe to Jennifer "J-Lo" Lopez.

Sullivan was born and raised in the Bronx. His father was a World War II veteran who remained with the Air National Guard and retired as a lieutenant colonel. His father's day job was as a New York City fireman, working Ladder 27 in the Bronx when that borough truly was burning down. His father continued a legacy, as his father and grandfather had also served New York City as firemen.

While his father was pulling people out of burning buildings, his mother stayed home and raised four kids—Kathleen, Rosemary, William, and the author. She gets a lot of the credit for any success the family has had.

Sullivan has worked for eighteen years in the New York State court system. He began as a court officer and then moved up the ranks to associate court clerk. Growing up in a turbulent time in the Bronx and working in the court system led to Sullivan's interest in crime, which eventually became the genesis for this book.

Sixteen years ago, Sullivan started as a journalist for the *New York Press*. At first he wrote about sports but soon began pitching crime stories, and that became his beat. He has worked for the *New York Post* for the last four years and claims it covers the city like no other paper.

He is the father of ten-year-old twins, Luisa and Olivia Sullivan, and claims that they are the true loves of his life.